Teach Yourself

VISUALLY™

Sewing

Teach Yourself VISUALLY™

Sewing

Visual®

by Debbie Colgrove

WILEY

Wiley Publishing, Inc.

Library of Congress Control Number: 2005939196

ISBN-13: 978-0-471-74991-2
ISBN-10: 0-471-74991-5

Printed in the United States of America

10 9 8 7 6 5 4 3 2

Book production by Wiley Publishing, Inc. Composition Services

Praise for the Teach Yourself VISUALLY Series

I just had to let you and your company know how great I think your books are. I just purchased my third Visual book (my first two are dog-eared now!) and, once again, your product has surpassed my expectations. The expertise, thought, and effort that go into each book are obvious, and I sincerely appreciate your efforts. Keep up the wonderful work!

—Tracey Moore (Memphis, TN)

I have several books from the Visual series and have always found them to be valuable resources.

—Stephen P. Miller (Ballston Spa, NY)

Thank you for the wonderful books you produce. It wasn't until I was an adult that I discovered how I learn—visually. Although a few publishers out there claim to present the material visually, nothing compares to Visual books. I love the simple layout. Everything is easy to follow. And I understand the material! You really know the way I think and learn. Thanks so much!

—Stacey Han (Avondale, AZ)

Like a lot of other people, I understand things best when I see them visually. Your books really make learning easy and life more fun.

—John T. Frey (Cadillac, MI)

I am an avid fan of your Visual books. If I need to learn anything, I just buy one of your books and learn the topic in no time. Wonders! I have even trained my friends to give me Visual books as gifts.

—Illona Bergstrom (Aventura, FL)

I write to extend my thanks and appreciation for your books. They are clear, easy to follow, and straight to the point. Keep up the good work! I bought several of your books and they are just right! No regrets! I will always buy your books because they are the best.

—Seward Kollie (Dakar, Senegal)

Credits

Acquisitions Editor
Pam Mourouzis

Project Editor
Donna Wright

Copy Editor
Elizabeth Kuball

Technical Editor
Louise Beaman

Editorial Manager
Christina Stambaugh

Publisher
Cindy Kitchel

Vice President and Executive Publisher
Kathy Nebenhaus

Interior Design
Kathie Rickard
Elizabeth Brooks

Cover Design
José Almaguer

Interior Photography
Matt Bowen

Special Thanks...

To the following companies for granting us permission to show photographs of their products:

- About.com
- Coats & Coats (www.coatsandclark.com)
- Fabric.com
- Husqvarna Viking Sewing Machines (www.husqvarnaviking.com)
- Pellon Consumer Products (www.pellon.com)
- Prym Consumer USA (www.dritz.com)
- The Snap Source, Inc. (www.snapsource.com)
- Simplicity Pattern Co. Inc. (www.simplicity.com)
- Singer Sewing Company (www.singer.com)
- Tacony Corporation (www.elna.com)
- Wild Ginger Software Inc. (www.wildginger.com)
- Wrights® (www.wrights.com)

About the Author

Sewing has always been a part of who Debbie Colgrove is and what she does in her spare time. She started sewing with her mother as a youngster, taking her first tailoring class at age 14. Since 1997, Debbie has been the sewing guide for About.com and continues to build an extensive library of sewing information on the website. As the former Web editor for *Sew News* magazine, she traveled extensively meeting sewing enthusiasts from all over the United States. She enjoys introducing sewing to children and adults through teaching sewing classes and individuals at charitable organizations such as 4-H clubs and charity sewing nights. Debbie serves on her local Home Economics advisory board and

also provides leader training for 4-H. She works with many sewing machine companies to keep the world abreast of the latest options available to home sewers. Debbie lives in upstate New York with her family.

Acknowledgments

After teaching many people to sew, I firmly believe that the book in your hands is the best possible learning tool for someone who wants to learn to sew. I can't thank the editors of this book enough for the opportunity to share the information that this book contains. A heartfelt thank you to the companies that shared their products and so much of their employees' time so that all the photos in this book could offer the best possible learning experience. I would also like to thank my husband and daughter for their patience and understanding when I lost track of time or deserted them.

I will never be able to thank my mother, Althea Triebel, for all the things she has done for me. But I would like to take this opportunity to thank her for teaching me to sew it correctly or rip it out (even when I balked) and for the endless hours of driving me to places to enhance my learning experiences.

Table of Contents

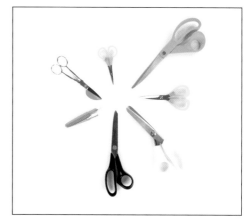

chapter 3 | Fabrics

chapter 4 | Lining, Interlining, and Interfacing

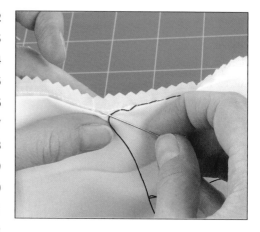

 **chapter 7** **Sewing Seams and Seam Finishes**

chapter 8 **Making Darts**

chapter 9 Sewing Facings and Edge Finishing

chapter 10 Sewing in Zippers

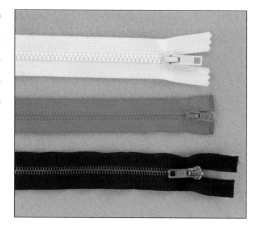

 **Adding Fasteners**

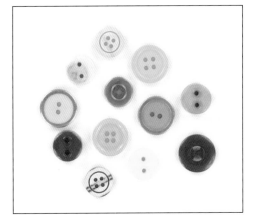

chapter 12 **Hemming Techniques**

chapter 13 Warm-Up Sewing Projects

chapter 14 More Sewing Projects

chapter 15 Using a Purchased Pattern

chapter 16 Expanding Your Horizons

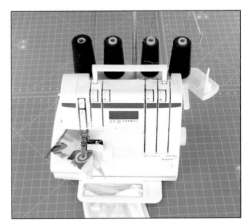

Getting to Know Your Sewing Machine

The largest financial investment you'll make in your sewing is the sewing machine. There are many choices of makes and models of new sewing machines from which to choose. Another option is to start with a used machine inherited from a relative or friend or bought at a sale. Whatever machine you're going to sew with, you need to learn what the parts are and what they do.

Experiment with your machine! Dive in and be creative. Having the machine malfunction when you start to sew can be very frustrating and distracts from the task at hand. The best way to avoid this is to be totally familiar with your machine. Save scraps of fabric when you're cutting out a project and use them to test your needle selection and machine settings.

SINGER

The Parts of a Sewing Machine

Sure, you can sew by hand, but a sewing machine makes the job a lot easier. The photos shown here might not exactly match your sewing machine, but they do show the basic parts that almost all sewing machines have. The location of the parts may vary on your machine.

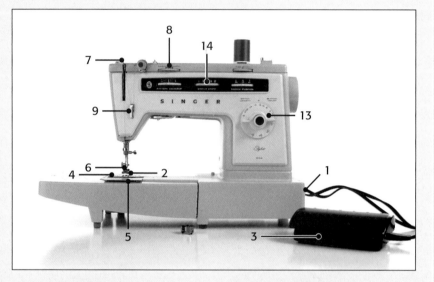

1. POWER SWITCH

This switch turns the power to your machine on and off.

2. PRESSER FOOT

The presser foot holds the fabric in place as you sew. Most machines have a way to adjust the pressure that this foot applies to the fabric. Presser feet come in a variety of shapes and sizes. Many of them are called specialty feet. Specialty feet are designed for one task but are often used for more than one job. For example, a zipper foot is used to insert zippers and is also commonly used to insert piping in a seam; however, there are also specialty feet for cording. Using a presser foot for more than one task saves money but may not be the easiest solution. Visit a local dealer and experiment with specialty feet whenever you find yourself frustrated with a particular task. The odds are in your favor that a special foot exists that will make the task easier.

3. FOOT PEDAL

Think of the foot pedal as the gas pedal. The pressure you apply controls the speed of the machine. Take time to experiment with the pressure you apply before you thread the machine.

4. THROAT PLATE

The throat plate protects the bobbin unit and usually has guides for seam allowances.

5. FEED DOGS

A strange name, but they work like dogs to feed the fabric under the needle to maintain an even stitch as you sew.

6. NEEDLE

Needles are available in different sizes with different points for different fabrics. The needle penetrates the fabric, taking the thread under the fabric and catching the bobbin thread to form stitches. If the needle is bent in the slightest way, the stitches will not form correctly. The needle size and type also play an important part in forming correct stitches. Holes in your fabric and skipped stitches are often caused by not using the correct needle.

7. TAKE-UP LEVER

This lever moves up and down as the machine operates, feeding thread to the needle.

8. UPPER TENSION REGULATOR

The upper tension regulator adjusts the amount of tension on the thread as it's fed to the needles. When the upper thread is too tight, you loosen the tension by turning the dial to the left or lower number. When the upper thread is too loose, you turn to the right or higher number to tighten it. A handy expression to help you remember which way to turn the dial is "Righty tighty, lefty loosey." Referring to your machine manual is the best way to make the correct adjustments.

9. THREAD GUIDES

The thread guides keep the thread flowing smoothly to the needle. Most machines have more than one thread guide, so don't skip any when threading your machine.

10. SPOOL HOLDER

Many machines offer a vertical and a horizontal option to hold the spool of thread. Vertical spool pins work best for thread that's wound evenly and horizontally on the spool. Horizontal spool pins work best for thread that is wound in a crisscross, diamond-forming type of pattern and is meant to feed over the end of the spool.

11. BOBBIN WINDER

The bobbin winder holds the bobbin and usually slides to a stop when the machine is in bobbin-winding mode. Refer to your manual for proper bobbin winding on your machine. An improperly wound bobbin can cause problems in obtaining a balanced stitch. Always use a slow, even speed on your sewing machine to obtain an evenly wound bobbin.

12. BALANCE WHEEL

The balance wheel turns as the machine runs. You can also use it to manually raise and lower the needle. On some machines, the inner wheel turns to disengage the machine for bobbin winding.

13. STITCH-LENGTH REGULATOR

The stitch-length regulator (see page 4) sets how much fabric is fed to the needle at a time, thereby determining the length of the stitches. The stitch-length regulator enables you to set the number of stitches per inch.

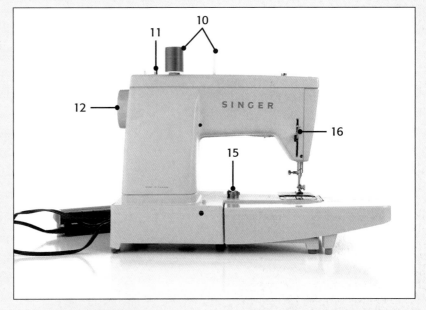

14. STITCH-WIDTH REGULATOR

Available on machines with zigzag and decorative stitches, the stitch-width regulator (see page 4) determines the distance the needle can travel from left to right. The amount of width available varies from one machine to the other.

15. BOBBIN AND BOBBIN CASE

The bobbin case holds the bobbin for the thread. The bobbin provides the thread for the underside of the stitching. It needs to be wound evenly in order for it to function properly. The bobbin case has a proper way to be threaded. Follow your machine manual to thread the bobbin properly in the bobbin case. There are adjustments on the bobbin case for the bobbin thread tension. Adjusting them is usually not necessary. You can see examples of bobbins in Chapter 6.

16. PRESSER-FOOT LIFTER

The presser-foot lifter enables you to lower and raise the presser foot. When the presser foot is raised, the tension on the upper tension regulator or tension discs is released. You should always thread the machine with this lever raised.

Sewing Machine Needles

The most often changed part of a sewing machine is the needle. The commonly accepted rule is that you should change the machine needle after every 10 to 12 hours of use. It's a good idea to have an assortment of machine needles on hand.

Because different types of needles are available, refer to your manual to purchase the correct type for your machine. The manual will also tell you how to insert the needle into the sewing machine correctly.

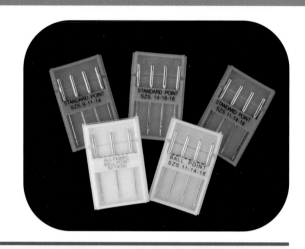

Needle Parts and Sizes

THE PARTS OF A NEEDLE

All sewing machine needles have the same basic components. Most home machine needles have a *flat* side and a *rounded* side at the top for proper insertion into the machine. The thread rides in a *groove* in the body of the needle as it goes to the *eye*.

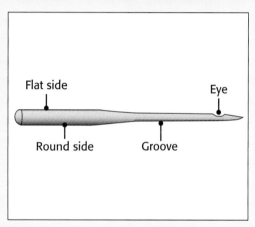

NEEDLE SIZES

Needle sizes are numbered using both European and American systems. Some companies label their needles with both systems, so for example you might see 60/8 or 120/19 on a package. In both systems, the higher the number, the thicker the needle.

Needle Size Conversion Chart			
European	*American*	*Fabric Weight*	*Fabric Examples*
60	8	light	very sheer fabric
65	9	light	lightweight, see-through fabric
70	10	light-medium	light T-shirt fabric
75	11	medium	blouse fabric

European	*American*	*Fabric Weight*	*Fabric Examples*
80	12	medium-heavy	lightweight denim
90	14	heavy	corduroy, suiting
100	16	heavy	medium-weight denim
100	18	very heavy	jeans
120	19	very heavy	canvas

Basic Types

Machine needles have a variety of points for different kinds of fabric and sewing tasks.

UNIVERSAL

Universal-point needles can usually be used for sewing both knit and woven fabrics. The point is slightly rounded, yet is still sharp enough to penetrate woven fabrics. These needles are sold in sizes 60/8 through 120/19.

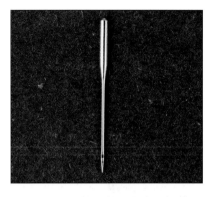

BALLPOINT

Ballpoint needles have slightly rounded tips to go between fabric fibers. They're used for knit fabrics. Ballpoint needles do not pierce fabric fibers, instead going between the fibers of knit fabrics. They are sold in sizes 70/10 through 100/16.

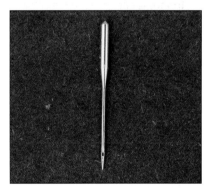

SHARPS

Sharp-point needles have—surprise!—very sharp points. They're used for woven fabrics. The sharp point enables the needle to penetrate the fabric. The piercing ability of these needles makes them especially well suited for making a perfect straight stitch, such as topstitching. Various companies use different names for sharp needles. You may find them packaged under the name Microtex (Schmetz) and Standard Point (Dritz). Sharp needles are sold in sizes 60/8 through 90/14.

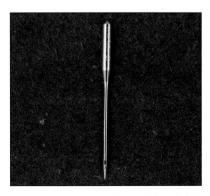

CONTINUED ON NEXT PAGE

Specialty Needles

As your sewing skills develop, you'll find yourself reaching for more-specialized needles.

TOPSTITCHING NEEDLE

Has an extra-sharp point, a larger eye, and a larger-than-normal groove to accommodate larger, topstitching thread. These needles also work well with metallic and delicate specialty thread. They're sold in sizes 80/12 through 100/16.

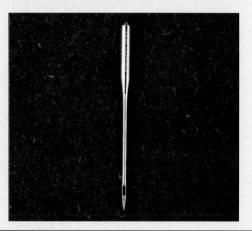

STRETCH NEEDLE

Used when a ballpoint needle won't make acceptable stitches in a knit fabric. This sometimes happens with fabric such as Lycra. They're sold in sizes 75/11 through 90.14.

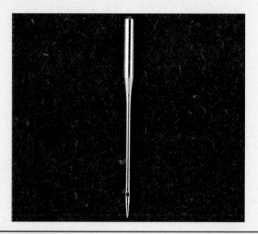

SELF-THREADING NEEDLE

A great choice for someone who has difficulty threading a needle. This general-purpose needle has a slot in one side of the eye for the thread to slide into the eye. They're sold in sizes 80/12 and 90/14.

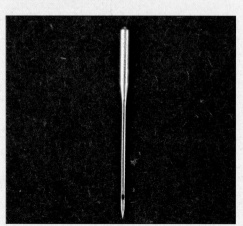

WING NEEDLE

Has a flared shank and is used to create decorative heirloom stitches. The needle creates decorative openwork stitching on tightly woven fabrics such as linen and fine batiste.

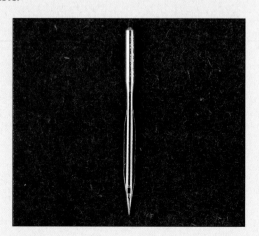

DENIM/JEANS NEEDLE

Especially well suited for heavy denim or similar weight fabric. It has an extra-sharp point for penetrating layers of heavy fabric. The eye of this needle is slim, but the shaft is strong. Denim needles are sold in sizes 70/10 through 110/18.

DOUBLE/TRIPLE NEEDLES

Multiple needles arranged on a crossbar with variable distances set between the needles. They allow perfectly spaced rows of stitching. The distance between the needles varies from 1.6mm to 8mm. They are labeled first with the needles' spacing distance and then the needles' size. Use these needles *only* with a throat plate with a large enough opening, and check your manual before using them. They're sold in sizes 80/12 through 100/16.

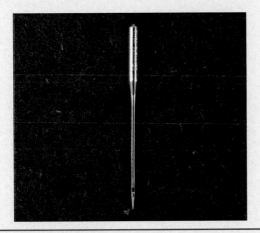

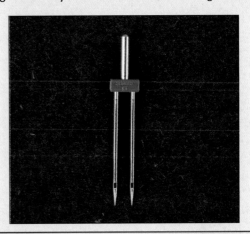

QUILTING NEEDLE

Has a tapered point to penetrate multiple layers of fabric and the cross-seams of quilts. They are sold in sizes 75/11 and 90/14.

EMBROIDERY NEEDLE

Has a large eye and is designed to protect decorative embroidery threads. They're sold in sizes 75/11 and 90/14.

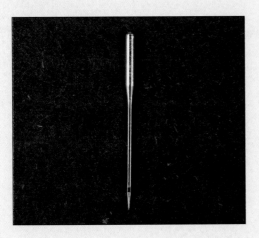

Sewing Machine Options

Before you buy a machine (new or used), consider how you're going to use it. If you just want to sew basic garments and home décor items, you don't need a heavy-duty machine. However, a machine with a wide variety of stitch options will enable you to create almost any item. Choose the correct needle with those stitches and you can sew almost any fabric.

Go to a local dealer for hands-on experience before you buy.

Basic Options

The basic options you need on a sewing machine to work with almost any fabric available today are:

STRAIGHT STITCH

The straight stitch is the most used stitch. You're going to depend on this stitch more than any other. Test the straight stitch on a variety of fabrics and be sure you like the results (a).

ZIGZAG STITCH

A zigzag is the most commonly used stitch for seam finishes and is often used for a stretch seam. The changes on stitch width and length should give you a variety of options (b).

BUTTONHOLE CAPABILITY

A variety of buttonhole options are available on different machines. Uniform stitches should be your goal in examining buttonholes (a).

STRETCH STITCH

A narrow zigzag can be used for a stretchable seam, but a built-in stretch stitch is a worthy investment (b).

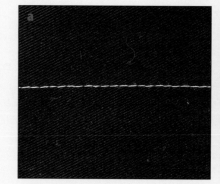

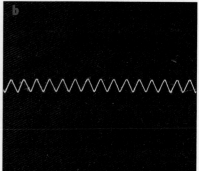

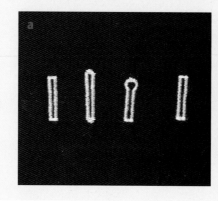

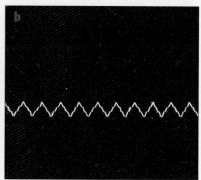

If you love fancy threadwork and love to embellish, it may be worth your investment to purchase a machine that has these capabilities. Talk to local sewing machine dealers and test-drive machines before you make the investment. Seeing how available options work can help you decide if it is something you want or need. Most dealers offer free classes with the purchase of a machine. These classes allow you to get the most out of your investment. A good dealer knows the equipment they sell and can answer questions when you have a problem. Any machine you buy should have customer service contact information.

The Manual

Whether your sewing machine is new or used, you *must* have the manual to maintain your machine properly and get the most out of it. Referring to the manual can save you hours of frustration.

You can purchase a manual or a copy of a manual for almost any older machine. The easiest way to obtain one is to visit a local sewing machine dealer. The following list can lead you to a local dealer or to a website where you can purchase a manual.

Purchase Manuals

MANUFACTURERS

Thousands of sewing machines are out there today. Have your machine's manufacturer and model number handy, if possible, when trying to track down a manual.

Company	Website	Phone
Baby Lock–Tacony	www.babylock.com	800-422-2952
Bernina USA	www.berninausa.com	800-405-2739
Brother Company	www.brother.com	800-284-4357
Elna	www.elna.com	800-848-3562
Husquavarna Viking	www.husqvarnaviking.com	800-446-2333
Janome	www.janome.com	800-631-0183
Pfaff	www.pfaff.com	800-997-3233
Riccar	www.riccar.com	800-995-9110
Sears Kenmore	www.kenmore.com	800-366-7278
Simplicity Sewing Machines	www.simplicitysewing.com	800-822-6691
Singer Company	www.singerco.com	800-474-6437
White Sewing Machines	www.whitesewing.com	800-446-2333

NON-MANUFACTURER SOURCES

If you can't get a manual from the manufacturer of your sewing machine, you might be able to purchase from one of the following sources:

- Shoppers Rule sells manuals for more than 15 brands of sewing machines. To enlist their assistance with your machine brand and model number, write to 2496 Starling Airport Road., Arnold, MO 63010; call 800-636-3460 or 314-287-9640; or visit www.shoppersrule.com.
- AllBrands.com sells many manuals. Call 866-255-2726 or visit www.allbrands.com.

Anyone who sews regularly dreams of having a room dedicated to sewing. The truth is, most people don't obtain that dream until later in life. You could easily let your sewing take over your home, but there are ways to rein it in.

Sewing can be addictive, too. Once you start a project, you might lose track of time; hours pass before you know it. Consider ergonomics wherever you set up your sewing machine. Proper height settings for your chair and table prevent back, neck, and arm fatigue.

TABLE

Many sewing cabinets and tables are available, but most people start at the kitchen table. You want a sturdy surface; a card table is not a suitable place to set up your sewing machine. The vibrations of the machine rattle the table and end up distracting from the task at hand. The kitchen or dining room table is usually the best solution. Most kitchen tables also provide a flat, smooth surface for cutting fabric.

CHAIR

The chair you use should be comfortable and provide support for your back. You should be able to reach the foot pedal on the floor and the bed of the sewing machine comfortably without putting undue stress on your back, legs, or shoulders. A good office chair usually has lumbar support and adjustable height.

LIGHT

Allow yourself plenty of light. Don't add excess eye fatigue by running your sewing machine with a burned-out lightbulb. They are relatively inexpensive and easy to replace. Many elaborate lighting solutions are on the market, and if you're going to sew for hours on end, they're worth the investment to prevent eye fatigue. Sewing strains the eyes, and the more light you provide, the less eye strain you'll feel. Lighted magnifying tools are also available. Visit your local sewing shop or lighting center when you're ready to invest in good lighting.

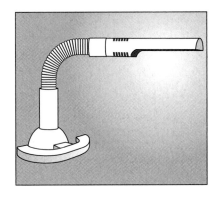

Basic Troubleshooting

A properly maintained machine can keep sewing and save you from costly repairs. Clean and oil your machine regularly as described in your machine manual. Before making any adjustments, be sure that you have the machine threaded correctly and the correct needle in the machine.

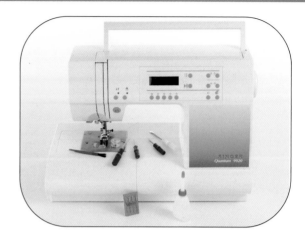

Common Problems

SKIPPING STITCHES

Skipped stitches are usually caused by having the wrong type of needle in the machine. If you're sewing a woven fabric, make sure you have a sharp needle in the machine. If you're sewing a knit fabric, try changing to a ballpoint needle. Before buying a stretch needle, test the stitch on a different knit fabric. If the machine is still skipping stitches, change the needle and try again. If it continues to skip stitches on different fabric and needle combinations, you may need to take the machine to a dealer for service, as the timing may be off. If the stitches are fine with a different knit fabric of a similar weight, purchase a stretch needle.

Inferior-quality thread can also cause skipped stitches. Try a different spool of thread before going to the repair shop.

INCORRECT TENSION SETTINGS

Refer to your manual to learn how to adjust the thread tension on your machine. Before you change the tension settings:

- Be sure you're using the correct needle.

- Be sure the machine is properly threaded, both the upper threading and the bobbin. Always thread the machine with the presser foot up so that the upper tension regulator is released and it accepts the thread.

- You can test that the tension discs are engaging by putting the presser foot down and gently pulling the needle thread to the rear of the machine. You should feel a difference between when the presser foot is down and when it is up.

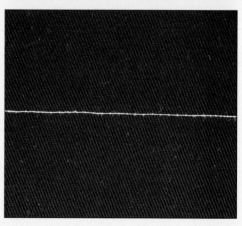

STITCHES PUCKER

You can usually remedy puckered stitches by loosening the stitch length.

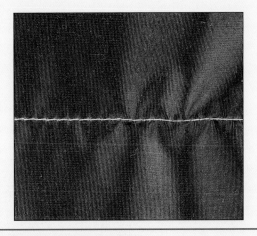

HOLES APPEAR IN FABRIC

If holes appear in your fabric, you are probably using a needle that's too large for the fabric. Try changing to a finer needle.

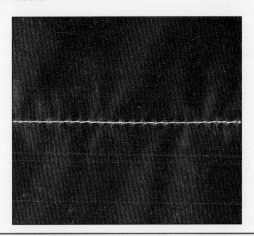

FABRIC ISN'T FEEDING

If the machine is stitching in one place and not feeding the fabric under the presser foot, make sure that the presser foot lever is all the way down and the feed dogs are up in the correct position. If both are in the correct position, you might have too much or not enough pressure on the presser foot. Refer to your manual for the correct adjustment.

BENT NEEDLES

Beginners often unknowingly pull the needle with the fabric, which causes the needle to bend. The slightest bend in the needle causes the machine to malfunction.

Be sure that the presser foot is up before pulling the fabric out of the machine.

Let the machine do the work. All you need to do is guide the fabric and allow the machine to feed the fabric through.

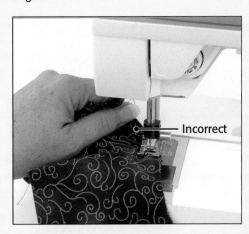

Incorrect

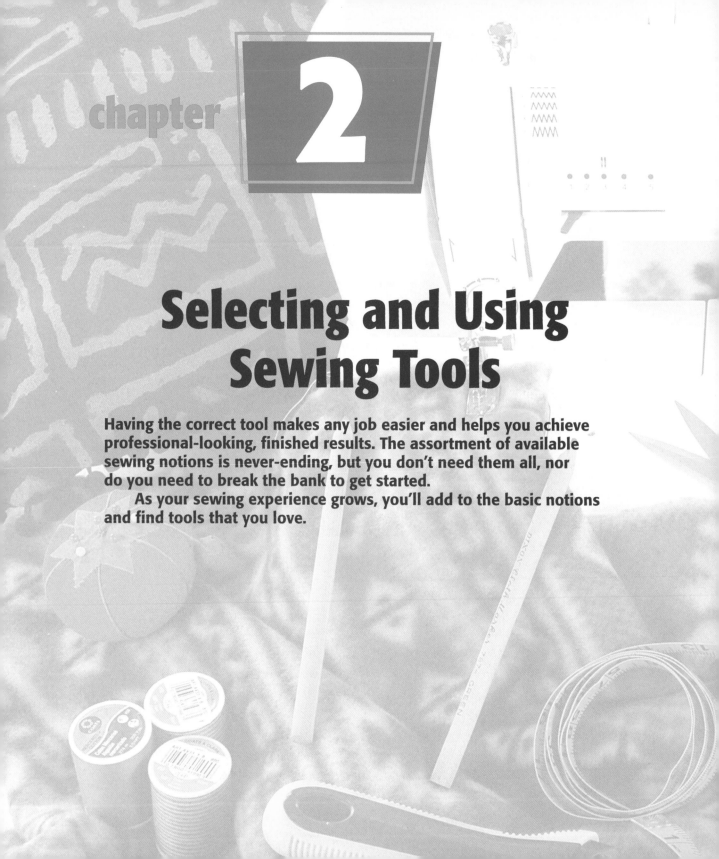

chapter 2

Selecting and Using Sewing Tools

Having the correct tool makes any job easier and helps you achieve professional-looking, finished results. The assortment of available sewing notions is never-ending, but you don't need them all, nor do you need to break the bank to get started.

As your sewing experience grows, you'll add to the basic notions and find tools that you love.

SINGER

Measuring Tools

Accurate, repeatable measurements are an important element to having pieces fit together as you sew clothing or craft items. The correct tools don't have to cost a fortune but are invaluable.

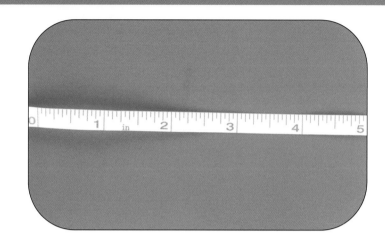

Types of Tools

TAPE MEASURE

Available almost anywhere, a tape measure is one of the most commonly used tools in sewing. A tape measure is pliable but does not stretch. Its pliability makes it perfect for taking body measurements and measuring curves.

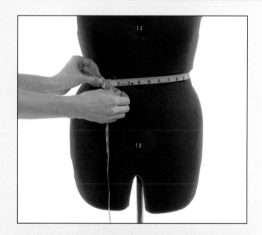

YARDSTICK

A yardstick is a measuring tool that most people have around the house. It's perfect for laying out patterns and measuring straight lengths of fabric as well as marking up hems from the floor.

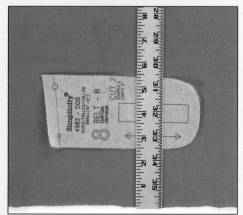

GAUGE

A gauge is a very inexpensive tool that enables you to create accurate hems, button spacing, and markings. The slide allows you to "set" the gauge and get perfect repeat measurements.

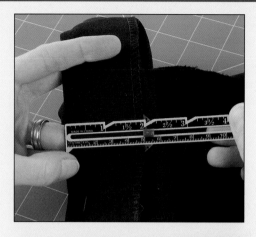

ROTARY RULER

A rotary ruler is not a necessary tool, but you may find it handy if you're going to be drafting squares and rectangles. The 1/8-inch increment markings allow for perfection when measuring. The vertical and horizontal markings enable you to create perfect squares and rectangles. These rulers are available in a variety of sizes in squares and rectangles. Although a 6 × 6-inch ruler is used in the photo, I've found that the 6 × 24-inch version is the most commonly used. You need a rotary cutting mat and a rotary cutter to use this tool as part of a cutting package. (See the "Cutting Tools" section for more information.)

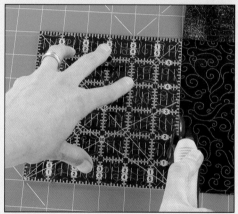

TIP

Whatever you're measuring, accuracy is the key to success. A measurement that is off by 1/4 inch might not seem like much, *until* you make that same 1/4-inch overage on four seams and have a full 2-inch excess.

Cutting Tools

Sharpness is the key element to any cutting tool. You want blades that will cut through fabric without shredding it.

1. DRESSMAKER SHEARS

Dressmaker shears are used for cutting out patterns. The long blade enables you to cut a smooth, continuous line. Bent-handle options are best for cutting out patterns because they allow you to keep the blades flat on the surface without lifting and moving the laid-out fabric and pattern.

2. NIPPERS

You use nippers to cut threads and for much of the clipping and trimming as you sew.

3. PINKING SHEARS

Trimming seam allowances with pinking shears is one of the many ways to prevent the fabric from fraying. Using pinking shears instead of a sewn seam finish eliminates bulk created by many sewing methods.

4. EMBROIDERY SCISSORS

Embroidery scissors are great to have on hand for trimming threads. In addition to having sharp blades with sharp points, they're small and compact, which is great when you're doing hand sewing.

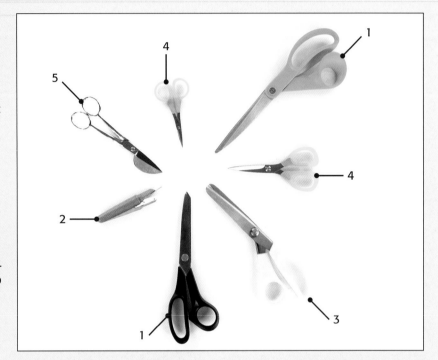

5. APPLIQUÉ SCISSORS

Appliqué or duckbill scissors are not a starter tool, but they are indispensable if you'll be doing appliqué work. The wide bottom blade enables you to trim with less likelihood of the blade cutting into the bottom fabric.

Rotary cutters and mats are not typical starter tools, but they're absolutely perfect for cutting squares, triangles, and rectangles. Quilters would be lost without these tools.

ROTARY CUTTERS

A rotary cutter has a thin round blade that rolls as it cuts. Using the rotary cutter in conjunction with a rotary ruler allows you to cut perfectly straight lines.

CUTTING MATS

Cutting mats are a base surface to protect your flat cutting surface. They're "self-healing" to the cuts made in them by the rotary cutter. Be sure to protect the surface that you're working on, especially surfaces that would be damaged by the rotary blade.

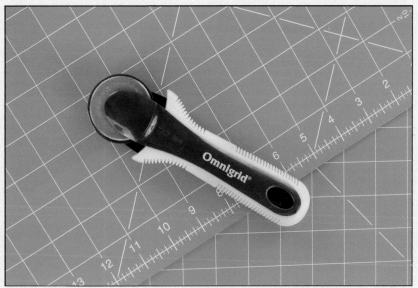

TIP

- Never use your fabric scissors to cut anything but fabric. Paper, plastic, and other items dull the blades, and before you know it you'll be shredding rather than cutting fabric. Keep household scissors on hand that have a different color handle than your sewing scissors so everyone in the house knows that one particular color handle is off limits.

- Sharp tips are an important element of any scissor. Dependable sharp points make it less likely to overcut when you're clipping and trimming seams.

- Scissors are available with spring-loaded blades and cushioned handles to help eliminate hand fatigue.

- Scissors come in a wide variety of shapes and sizes. Two basic scissors will get you started: 7-inch to 9-inch dressmaker shears and nipping scissors.

Thread

Thread comes in a wide variety of weights and types. This section tells you all about the different choices and points out some important things to keep in mind as you select thread for a project.

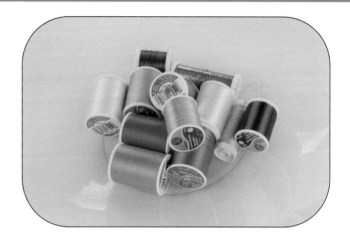

Things to Consider

THREAD QUALITY

The most important aspect of thread is quality. Your sewing machine depends on a consistent feed of thread to form a consistent stitch. As the thread travels through the machine, it goes though guides, tension discs, the needle groove, and the needle eye, all of which put stress on the thread to hold a consistent tension. If the thread is of poor quality (composed of small knots, inconsistent thickness, and loose fibers), it will be impossible for the machine to maintain consistent tension, causing breaking thread, poor-quality stitches, and weak seams.

THREAD FIBER

Cotton and polyester threads are the most readily available. Many people think that if you're sewing cotton fabric, you want cotton thread. Actually, the choice is just a matter of preference.

THREAD WEIGHT

Thread is available in a variety of weights. Due to different labeling system for thread weights between the United States and Europe, your best bet is to trust your fingers when choosing thread weight. Use thinner-weight thread for thinner fabrics and heavier weights for heavy fabrics.

THREAD COLOR

On print fabric, you want to match the most dominant color. When a perfect color match is not available, choose the slightly darker option over a slightly lighter option as thread tends to sew in a shade lighter.

CONTINUED ON NEXT PAGE

FAQ

Can thread shrink?

The less expensive the thread, the greater the likelihood that it will shrink, causing puckered seams after one washing. Spending a bit more on high-quality thread protects the time investment you put in to everything you sew.

Does thread get old?

Thread does age. Just because a color thread found in an old sewing box will match doesn't make it worth using. Test the strength and stability of old thread before you use it by stretching a length and testing it for breaking. Store thread out of direct sunlight and dusty environments.

All-purpose thread is made with a polyester core that is covered with cotton. It's available in a variety of weights and can be used for almost any sewing project.

Mercerized cotton thread is another construction thread for sewing natural-fiber fabric. It is smooth, lustrous, and 100 percent dyeable.

Embroidery and embellishment thread is available in rayon, polyester, and metallic fibers. This beautiful thread can add artistry to anything you're sewing, but it doesn't have the strength you want for basic construction.

Large cones of serger thread are sold for sewing with a serger. This thread is thinner than normal thread to eliminate excess bulk in a serged seam. Although using serger cones with a thread stand might seem economical, remember that this thread does not have the same strength as regular thread.

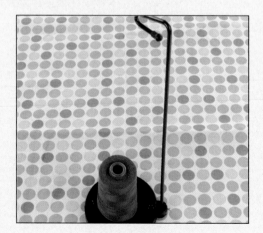

Hand-sewing needles are an inexpensive investment. A wide variety of them on hand allows you to have the type of needle available when you need it. As with threads and straight pins, hand-sewing needles come in a variety of weights, lengths, and sizes.

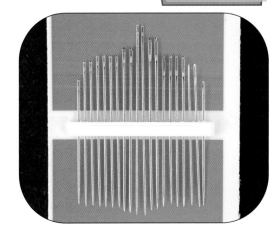

TYPES OF NEEDLES

The size of the eye of the needle corresponds with the size of the needle. Large-eyed needles are easy to thread, and your first impulse may be to take the easy way out. Remember, though, that the large eye is going to go through the fabric you're sewing and may leave holes if you're working with a fine fabric. Use fine needles for fine fabric. Save those large-eyed needles for craft projects and heavyweight fabric.

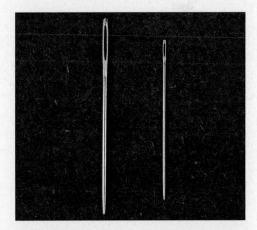

NEEDLE THREADERS

Needle threaders make using a small-eyed needle easy. Many assortment packages come with a needle threader or combination needle threader and magnifier. The needle threader may become your best friend. It's a simple way to thread any hand-sewing needle.

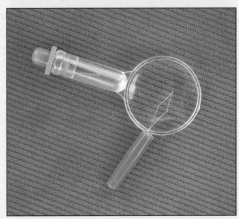

Straight Pins and Pincushions

Straight pins are available in a variety of lengths, thicknesses, and heads. You use them to hold fabric together temporarily before stitching it on a sewing machine. To keep your pins in one place, make sure that you have a pincushion or two.

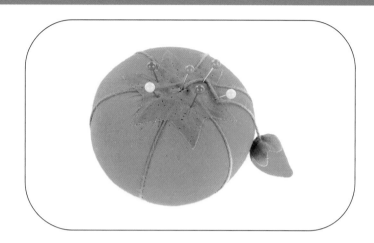

Work with Straight Pins

You want the weight of the pin you choose to work with the fabric you're using. A thin, sheer fabric requires a thin, straight pin. In contrast, a thick upholstery fabric requires a thick, strong straight pin. Trying to use a thin, straight pin on thick fabric causes it to bend, rendering it unusable.

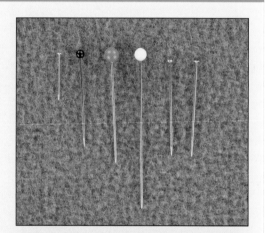

Always use clean, smooth straight pins. *Never* place pins in the seam line or sew over them with your sewing machine. The photo shows a seam that's been pinned properly. (See more information on sewing seams in Chapter 7.)

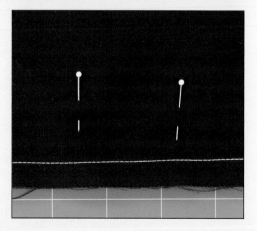

TOMATO PINCUSHION

Everyone has seen the standard tomato pincushion. Did you know that the dangling strawberry is filled with emery for sharpening needles? Emery is the same material that coats fine sandpaper and emery boards. The tomato is filled with wood sawdust and sometimes wool roving or wool yarn. See the intro photo on the previous page.

DECORATIVE PINCUSHIONS

If you like to sew on the run or have sewing materials in your living spaces, you can use decorative pincushions. They range from country chairs to sterling silver figures (see photo on this page). Many decorative pincushions don't hold a large number of pins, but they'll hold a few sewing needles.

MAGNETIC PINCUSHION

Magnetic pincushions are also available. Stainless steel straight pins are not magnetic and will not stay on a magnetic pincushion. If you're sewing near computer equipment and storage media, keep the magnet away from the computer equipment (computer equipment can become damaged by magnets).

Marking Tools and Seam Rippers

Accurate marking can make or break your sewing project. Most pattern markings from a purchased pattern can be transferred using dressmaker's carbon and a tracing wheel. The combination of dressmaker's carbon and a tracing wheel allows you to mark two pieces of fabric at the same time. With these markings you can match darts on both sides of a garment, line up seams, join parts of a garment at the correct location, and keep a garment balanced.

Although not a marking tool, a seam ripper can help you remove stitches without damaging your fabric.

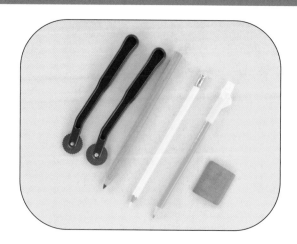

TRACING WHEELS

There are two commonly found tracing wheels. One is smooth and one is spindled. Using the smooth wheel causes a continuous solid line of marking (a). Using a spindled tracing wheel causes a dotted line (b). For more information on using marking tools, see Chapter 6.

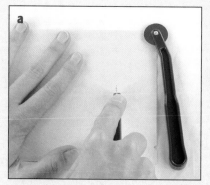

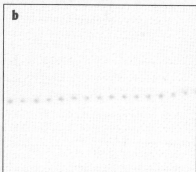

VANISHING PENS AND TAILOR'S CHALK

Vanishing pens are a simple way to make a temporary mark. Always test the pen on a fabric scrap before marking your project to ensure that the ink will disappear. Read the cautions on the package of the pen you purchase (a).

Tailor's chalk is an inexpensive option for temporary marking that will not crush the fibers of your fabric. Velvet and velour are examples of fabrics on which you might want to use tailor's chalk (b).

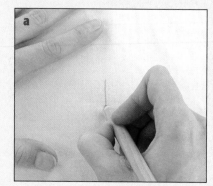

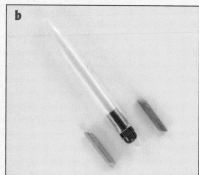

SEAM RIPPERS

Seam rippers are tools that you love to hate. You hope you won't have to use one because it means removing stitches, but even the most experienced sewer knows that it's inevitable. Using a seam ripper is the safest way to remove stitches without accidentally cutting your fabric.

Seam rippers come small and large, inexpensive and expensive, lighted, and in any other form a company can devise.

The most commonly used seam ripper has a fine tip and a cover that protects the blade, doubling as a handle.

Larger, heavier seam rippers are perfect for removing heavy stitches and heavy thread from items such as upholstery and canvas.

See more on how to remove stitches with a seam ripper on page 77.

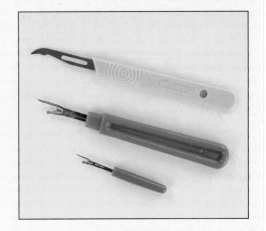

TIP

The dollar or two that a seam ripper costs is well worth the investment. My grandmother's sewing box contained a variety of razor blades that she used to remove stitching. Razor blades are not a safe way to remove stitching. They're apt to cut the fabric and ruin your project.

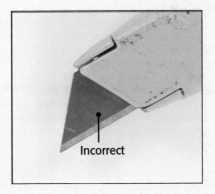

Incorrect

Ironing and Pressing

Ironing and pressing are important elements of obtaining professional-looking results. You can use a normal household iron and ironing board—there's no need to go out and buy expensive equipment to begin sewing.

Temperature settings are usually marked on your iron; use the appropriate temperature for the fabric you're pressing. The safest way to prevent accidents with your iron is to test your settings on scraps of fabric before pressing a project.

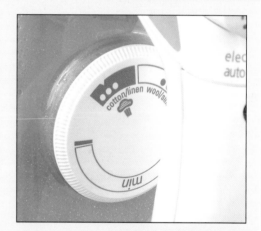

A press cloth is often used to protect fabric from getting singed or shiny. Many types of press cloths are available. To use one, follow the directions on the package of the cloth you purchase.

When you sew and press, you move the iron on a flat surface. Your purpose is to set stitches and create shape in the fabric. When you iron, you are gliding the iron to remove wrinkles. Ironing as you are sewing can move the threads of the fabric and distort the grain of the fabric. **Always press when you sew.**

Pressing aids are available for all kinds of construction. A seam that is not well pressed screams "homemade." Special tools for pressing hard to get at seams eliminate an unprofessional finished result.

Humans have curves and so do our clothes. Pressing the curves into the garment helps to achieve complimentary clothing.

SLEEVE BOARD

A sleeve board is a miniature ironing board for pressing narrow tube seams, such as a sleeve, without causing creases where you don't want them.

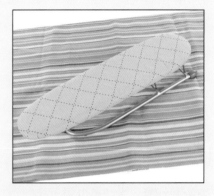

SEAM ROLL

A seam roll serves a similar purpose but can be moved further in to tube-type areas, as there is no base to stop your movement.

PRESSING HAM

A pressing ham helps you obtain perfectly pressed curved seams and darts.

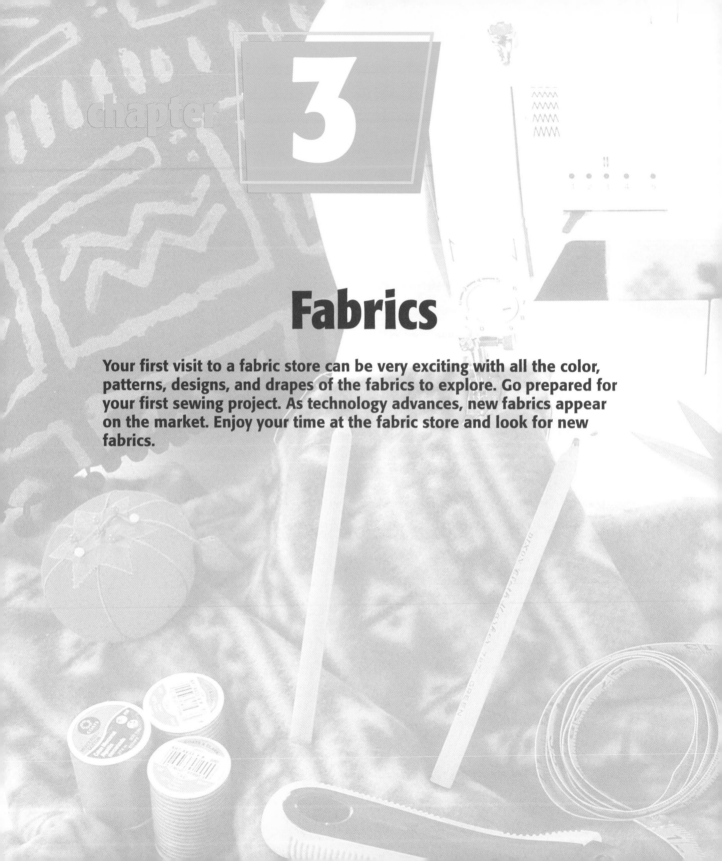

chapter 3

Fabrics

Your first visit to a fabric store can be very exciting with all the color, patterns, designs, and drapes of the fabrics to explore. Go prepared for your first sewing project. As technology advances, new fabrics appear on the market. Enjoy your time at the fabric store and look for new fabrics.

SINGER

One of the easiest fabric to work with is woven 100 percent cotton. Cotton is easy to work with because it "sticks" to itself without sliding, making managing the fabric easier than most other fabrics. Cotton blends are also a great choice for beginners. The fibers of the fabric react similarly to 100 percent cotton.

Types of Fabrics

100 PERCENT COTTON

Mass merchants that carry fabric, as well as fabric stores, usually have a wide variety of prints and solids available in 100 percent cotton. Because quilters use 100 percent cotton fabric, this section of the store is sometimes called the "Quilter's Corner" or "Quilter's Wall." The fabrics are usually arranged by color families. The variety of prints and solids is extensive.

WOVEN FABRICS

Beyond 100 percent cotton, other woven fabrics should be your first choice for beginner sewing projects. Allow yourself time to get totally comfortable with your sewing machine before working with knits and stretchy fabrics. They aren't difficult to work with once you have a firm grasp of how the sewing machine feeds the fabric. But working with knits before you have this knowledge can lead to puckered and distorted seams.

POLAR FLEECE

Polar Fleece is a great fabric to experiment with. It does not fray, so seam finishes are not required. It is available in a huge variety of prints and solids. Each year, new prints are introduced.

ADVANCED FABRICS

Slippery fabrics such as satins, sheers, and Lycra as well as super-stretchy fabrics require a bit of experience. If you're eager to work with these types of fabrics, look for remnants and purchase some at a bargain price. Practice seams and other techniques you want to achieve with the fabric before you invest in full yardage.

TIP

Making doll clothes, even if you donate them somewhere, allows you to practice various techniques using remnants of fabric. Choose full-size doll clothes patterns with darts, gathers, and closures to practice regular clothing construction techniques. Does any little girl ever have enough clothes for her doll?

Fabric Characteristics

When you look at fabric, you will learn to make note of its various characteristics. The color is the first thing that will draw your attention. Matching the print on the fabric may be cause for you to purchase more than you originally planned. The process used to make the fabric will determine the stretchability. The fibers will not only change the durability and feel of the fabric but the draping, laundering, and more.

Characteristics

SELVEDGE

All fabric has a *selvedge.* The selvedge is the bound area of the fabric on the edges. The selvedge may also contain information. Color dots show the colors used in the fabric. The manufacturer's name might also be printed on the selvedge. Many home decorating fabrics have a marking to show the print repeat. This is helpful in matching prints and deciding how much extra fabric you'll need to purchase.

Print repeat marking

WOVEN VS. KNIT

Most fabric is either woven or knitted. Woven fabric (a) is composed of threads running horizontally and vertically, weaving in and out to form the fabric. Knit fabric (b) is composed of threads that form loops and allow the fabric to stretch.

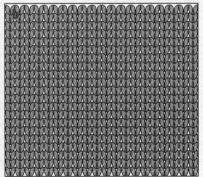

GRAIN

- **Fabric grain** is the way the thread that makes up the fabric travels.

- **Lengthwise grain** runs horizontal to the selvedge or the length of the fabric. Lengthwise grain is usually used to run the length of a garment (a).

- **Crosswise grain** runs perpendicular to the lengthwise grain. Crosswise grain usually runs across or around a garment (b).

- **Bias grain** is the grain that runs at a 45-degree angle to the straight grains of fabric (c). Bias hangs differently and bends differently from straight grains. Bias tape is cut from the bias grain and has more "give" when enclosing round areas.

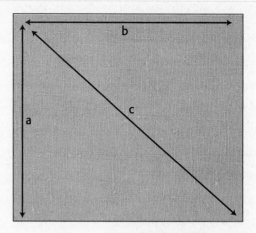

NAP

Nap refers to the way the pile of the fabric lays. You'll find nap on any fabric with a pile finish, such as velvet or terrycloth (a). You'll need to follow a with-nap layout in pattern directions for this type of fabric so that all pieces are cut in the same direction.

With-nap directions are also used for fabrics with a one-way design (b). Failing to follow the with-nap layout can result in the pattern being in one direction on one part of the item you're sewing and the opposite direction on the other side of the item.

TIP

- Plaid and striped fabrics require special layout using the with-nap directions.

- Don't choose a striped or plaid fabric for your first sewing project. Once you understand how pieces fit together, you'll find it much easier to match the design in stripes or plaids.

Test Fiber Content

Many bargain tables and fabric remnants do not have the bolt end information that tells you the fabric's fiber content. Don't despair—you can get a good idea of what the fibers are by doing a burn test, which will help you know how to care for the fabric.

Burn Test

No special equipment is needed to do a burn test. Always use caution and have water readily available when doing a burn test.

Hold a small piece of fabric with tweezers over a sink. Gently bring a flame to the edge of the scrap of fabric, paying attention to the smell as well as to how the fiber burns.

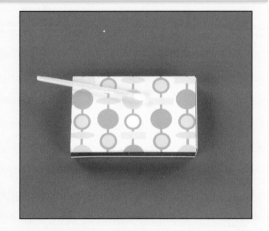

Fiber	Burn Results
Acetate or triacetate	Catches the flame and burns quickly. The melt of the fibers is a brittle, black bead. Produces a vinegar odor.
Acrylic	Catches the flame and burns quickly, producing a sputtering flame. The melted fibers are hard, black, irregular beads. Produces a bitter, irritating odor.
Cotton or linen	As soon as they make contact with the flame, these fibers burn. They burn very quickly and leave a light, wispy ash. Produces an odor like burning paper.
Nylon	Burns evenly with a blue and orange flame. Melts into a hard, gray-brown to black bead. Produces a celery odor.
Polyester	Burns with an orange flame and sputters as it burns. The melt produces a shiny, hard, round bead. Produces a sweet odor.
Rayon	Burns quickly and leaves a very slight ash. Produces an odor similar to burning leaves.
Silk	Usually burns, but not with a steady flame. Produces an ash that is easily crumbled. Produces an odor similar to singed hair.
Wool	Produces a steady flame but is difficult to keep burning. Produces an odor similar to singed hair.

Fabric is sold by the yard or by the meter, depending on where you are. Portions of yards and meters are perfectly acceptable, so you only have to purchase the amount of fabric you need.

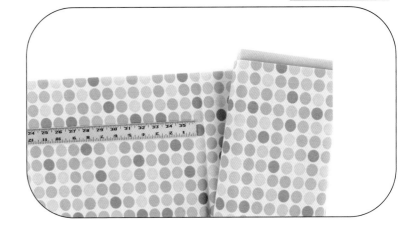

Buy the Right Amount

Everything you sew will require a certain amount of fabric. Patterns specify the amount of fabric you will need. (See more information on pattern envelope information in Chapter 15.) Purchase the amount you need according to the pattern you are following unless you will be adding length, then buy extra. Watch as your fabric is cut to be sure it is being cut straight. The inch that is crooked may cause you to not have enough, and you should receive the amount you want to buy.

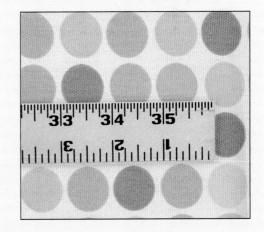

Here's a handy chart to understand how many inches of fabric you'll buy for each portion of a yard.

Yards	Inches
⅛ yard	4½ inches
¼ yard	9 inches
⅓ yard	12 inches
½ yard	18 inches
⅝ yard	22½ inches
⅔ yard	24 inches
¾ yard	27 inches
1 yard	36 inches

TIP

Many stores have precut "fat quarters." These pieces are ¼ yard but are not cut in the conventional method. The store cuts a ½-yard piece and then cuts it in half at the fold so that you have a square ¼ yard rather than the typical ¼ yard. These pieces are an excellent way to have a variety of fabrics on hand for small projects, quilting, and appliqués.

Unless it is precut, as is the case with fabric remnants, fabric is usually shipped to stores folded and wrapped on cardboard bolts. The end of the bolt has all the information you need about the fabric you're purchasing.

What You'll Find

Writing down the bolt end information to store with your fabric is a wise idea. Here is the information you're likely to find:

- Fiber content
- Style number and/or name
- Care information
- Manufacturer

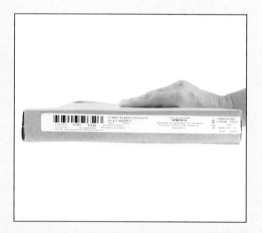

Special finishes may also be noted on the bolt end. You might find other information as well:

- **Flame retardant:** Required by law for making children's pajamas.
- **Permanent press:** Fabric that has been treated with a special finish to prevent wrinkling.
- **Preshrunk:** May be marked on the bolt, but it is wise to preshrink the fabric even if it marked as preshrunk.

TIP

Not all fabric is found on typical cardboard bolts. Fabric stores also have round tubes. A hang tag should accompany this fabric with the information that you would find on the bolt ends. Occasionally, there is a sticker on the end of the tube with the information.

Before you start to cut your fabric or interfacing for a project, you want to preshrink and press it.

PRESHRINK

Preshrink your fabric by washing and drying it the same way you will wash and dry the finished garment. If the fabric is loosely woven or prone to fraying, zigzag the single layer of the fabric's raw edge so that you don't lose fabric to the preshrinking process.

Preshrink interfacing and notions, such as lace, zippers, bias tape, and trims, by soaking them in a sink full of warm water. Blot out the excess water by rolling the interfacing in a towel. You can machine-dry them by placing them in a stocking to prevent tangles and damage.

Do not machine-dry fusible interfacing. The heat of the dryer will deteriorate the fusing capabilities and leave residue on the interior of your dryer.

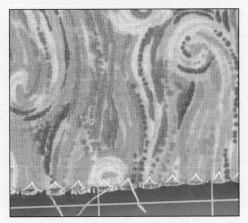

PRESS

When the fabric is dry, you press it. Pressing the fabric eliminates wrinkles, which allows the fabric to lay flat and ensures accuracy when you lay out the pattern.

Use the temperature setting on the iron that is appropriate to the fabric you're pressing. Use steam if necessary. Press the fabric in the direction of the lengthwise and crosswise grain to prevent warping the grain of the fabric. Use a spray bottle with water on stubborn wrinkles. *Do not stretch the fabric with the iron.* Fold the fabric as it came off the bolt, matching the selvedges. Read more about ironing and pressing in Chapter 2.

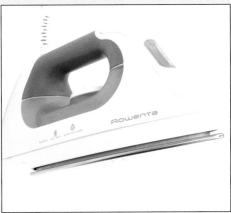

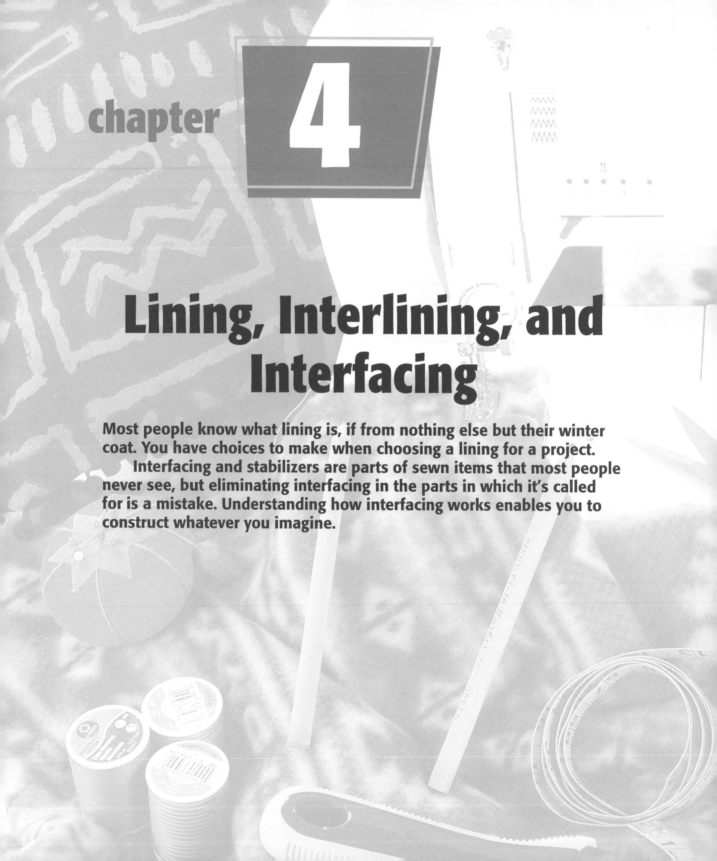

chapter 4

Lining, Interlining, and Interfacing

Most people know what lining is, if from nothing else but their winter coat. You have choices to make when choosing a lining for a project.
Interfacing and stabilizers are parts of sewn items that most people never see, but eliminating interfacing in the parts in which it's called for is a mistake. Understanding how interfacing works enables you to construct whatever you imagine.

SINGER

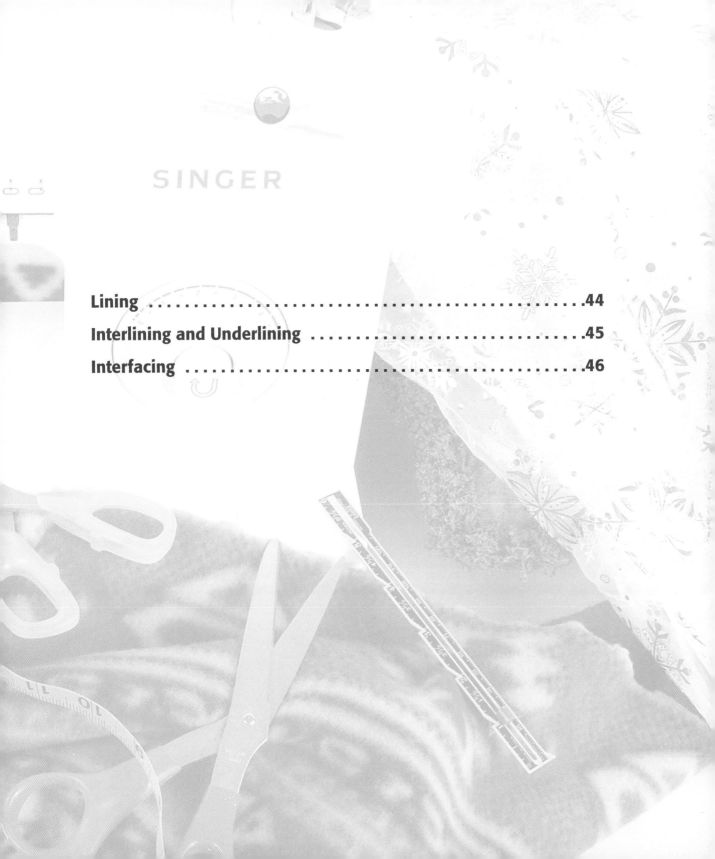

Lining

Lining is the inner fabric of a sewn item. You use a lining when you don't want the seams and construction of the outer layer to show. Since lining a garment can be a daunting task, practice lining a tote bag before attempting to line a garment.

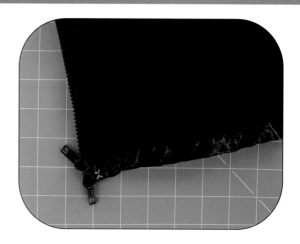

Choosing a Lining

Choosing lining isn't complex. The outer fabric and the lining must accept the same cleaning method. You'll need to choose a lining fabric with a weight that's compatible with the outer fabric. The lining fabric should be smooth and should not interfere with the way the outer fabric hangs. The color of the lining fabric should complement the outer fashion fabric of whatever you're making.

When selecting a lining for a garment, you may want to check the bolt end of the fabric for an "anti-static" finish. This prevents the garment from building static as you move. The most common choices for lining fabrics are silk, satin, sateen, crepe, batiste, taffeta, blouse-weight fabrics, cotton blend, and cotton as shown in the photo.

When in doubt, try to find a ready-made garment similar to what you want to make and examine the manufacturer's lining choice.

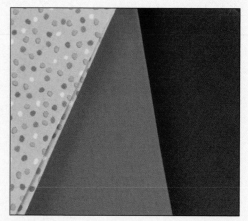

Interlining and underlining are two terms you'll see as your sewing skills advance. Learning about them helps you explore the possibilities that exist as you become creative and experiment with your own ideas.

INTERLINING

Interlining is an unseen interior layer of a garment. Its purpose is to add warmth. It is not used to add shape. Be aware that you do not want to add too much bulk when choosing an interlining fabric. Common choices for interlining are blanket fabrics, wool, felt, and fleece as shown in the photo.

UNDERLINING

Underlining is a layer of fabric that is stay-stitched to the outer fabric and then sewn as one fabric, unlike lining, which is constructed on its own and then joined to the rest of the garment. Not using underlining on a sheer fabric (a) allows seams to show through the fabric.

Underlining gives body to the outer fabric and allows the seams and construction details to be hidden when the outer fabric is see-through (b).

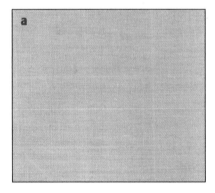

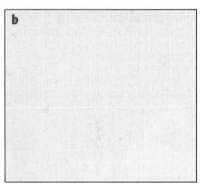

Interfacing

Interfacing gives body and adds shape to parts of a garment. Your creativity can abound once you know the varieties available and how they work with fabric. Interfacing is used in collars, cuffs, facings, and buttonhole areas to add structure to garments.

Interfacing comes in a wide variety of weights, in fusible and sew-in form, and in woven, knitted, and non-woven form.

Interfacing Weight

You choose interfacing weight by the outer fabric and what you're trying to achieve with the interfacing. When interfacing garments, in areas such as collars, cuffs, and facings, you'll usually choose an interfacing that is very slightly lighter than your outer fabric and adds the desired stiffness. However, an exceptionally crisp, stiff fabric may want a light interfacing, just enough to give the interfaced area a bit more body than the rest of the garment.

Test the "feel" of the fabric and interfacing together on a sample before sewing your garment or project.

If you're interfacing a fabric that you want to have an abundance of body, such as a medium-weight fabric to make a purse, you'll choose a stiff interfacing that will "harden" the fashion fabric. The photos show bags made out of the exact same fabric. The interfaced bag (a) stands on its own while the bag without interfacing (b) is floppy and lacks body. Interfacing allows you to stiffen a fabric and expand the possible uses for that particular fabric.

Woven, Knitted, and Non-Woven

Woven, knitted, and non-woven interfacing is a matter of choice; however, knitted interfacing is best to use with knit fabrics to maintain the stretchiness of the knit fabric.

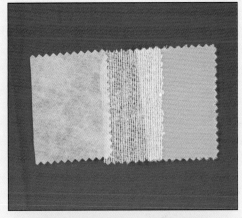

The fiber content of the interfacing you choose does not have to match the fabric you're using it with, but it does need to have the same care requirements, because it will be part of the finished garment.

Interfacing is relatively inexpensive. When in doubt, ask the store clerk for assistance or buy two interfacings closest to the weight you think you want. Test them with scraps of fabric.

CONTINUED ON NEXT PAGE

Fusible Interfacing

Fusible interfacing fuses to your fashion fabric with the heat of an iron. Before fusing the interfacing to the fabric, don't treat the fashion fabric with fabric softener, and wash out any manufacturer chemicals or sizing.

Fusible interfacing adds a bit more rigidity than the same weight of a sew-in type of interfacing, once it is fused to fabric. The fusing process adheres the interfacing directly to the fabric, and the "gluing" process adds extra stiffness.

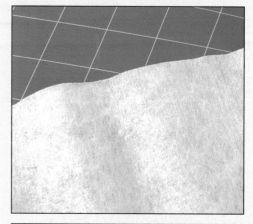

Fusible interfacing comes by the bolt and in packaged precut amounts. When on the bolt, it usually has a plastic sheet wrapped with the interfacing. Read the interfacing instructions or how to fuse before using it. Most people find fusible interfacing the easiest form to work with. Whatever your choice, experiment on fabric samples before you fuse to your sewing project.

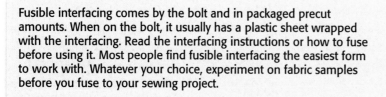

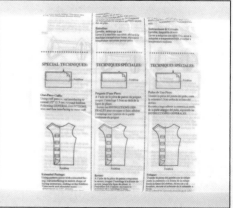

When you have enough fabric, fusing the interfacing *before* cutting out pattern pieces is easier. Then cut the pattern pieces as you would plain fabric.

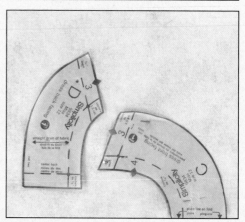

Sew-in Interfacing

Sew-in interfacing is sewn into the seam allowance of a garment or other project. It moves with the fabric and offers slightly less stiffness than the same weight of fusible interfacing. There are multiple ways to sew in this type of interfacing.

The most commonly used interfacing is light to medium weight. When sewing in this weight interfacing, baste the interfacing to the wrong side of the cut fabric, just outside the regular seam line within the seam allowance. Trim away the extra interfacing in the seam allowance, outside the basting line to eliminate bulk in the seam lines.

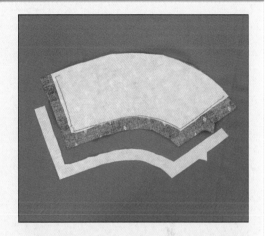

Heavyweight sew-in interfacing requires a different technique at seams to prevent multiple layers of interfacing and too much bulk as described below.

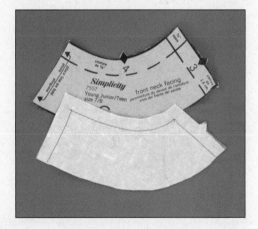

The pattern pieces are cut out of the interfacing. The seam allowance is cut away (a).

The seam lines are butted to each other and are sewn together using a wide, long, zigzag stitch (b).

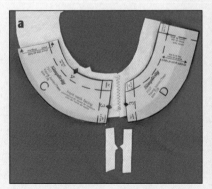

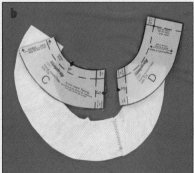

5

Hand Sewing

Almost everyone prefers the speed of a sewing machine, but there are times when hand sewing is the way to achieve a desired result. Knowing how to make stitches and when to use them makes hand sewing an enjoyable pastime. Save your hand sewing for car rides and television viewing.

SINGER

Threading a Hand-Sewing Needle

Unless you have 20/20 vision, threading a sewing needle can be a trying task. But it doesn't have to be. Using a needle threader can make it easy for you to thread the needle.

Thread the Needle

1. Using the size needle that is appropriate for your fabric, cut a piece of thread approximately 18 inches long. Longer thread will tangle; shorter thread is apt to come out of the needle. Cut the end of the thread on an angle.

2. Push the wire end of the threader through the eye of the needle.

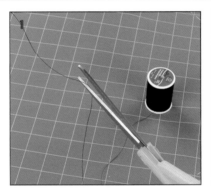

3. Place the thread through the loop of the wire.

4. Pull the wire back through the needle eye, and remove the thread from the needle threader wire.

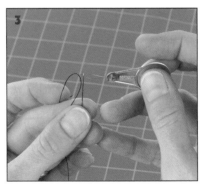

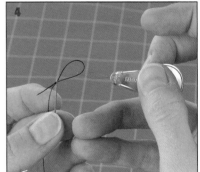

The size of the knot will depend on the weave of the fabric you're sewing. A coarse, open-weave fabric requires a large knot that prevents the knot from sliding through the fabric. A thin, tightly woven fabric requires a small knot that won't show through the fabric.

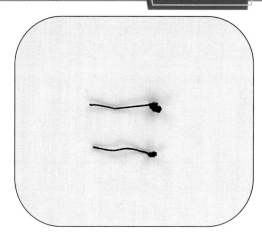

Knot the Thread

1 Place the end of the thread on the palm side of your index finger, with the end of the thread toward your body. Hold it in place with your thumb.

2 Bring the thread under your index finger, around your finger until it slips under your thumb.

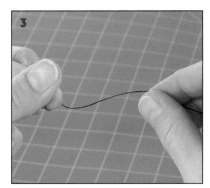

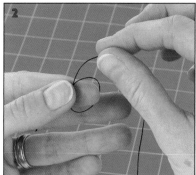

3 Roll the thread between your thumb and index finger with your thumb rolling the thread off the end of your index finger, while rolling across the bottom of your thumb.

4 Allow the end of your middle finger to help hold the thread between the bottom of your middle finger and the top of your index finger. Pull the thread with your right hand as you use your thumbnail and index finger to snug the knot down to the end of the thread.

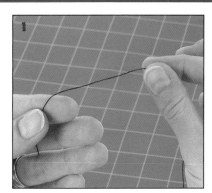

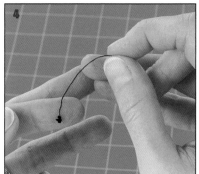

Double Thread or Single Thread

A double-threaded needle may seem like it's easier to work with, but your finished results may not be what you were aiming for.

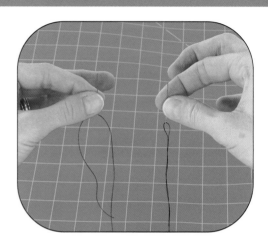

WHEN TO USE A SINGLE THREAD

Use a single thread for most hand sewing. If you don't want the hand stitches to be seen, you want the thinness of a single thread (a).

A single thread can be tricky to keep the needle threaded. Work with the thread doubled except for a few inches from the knot. Gently pull the thread through the needle after sewing a few inches to move the doubled thread up toward the needle (b).

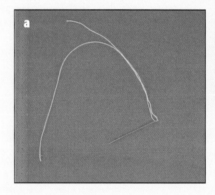
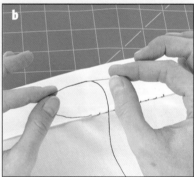

WHEN TO USE A DOUBLE THREAD

Use a double thread whenever you want strong, durable stitches (a). Sewing on a button or a fastener is typically done with a double-threaded needle (b). In this case, both threads are included in the knot.

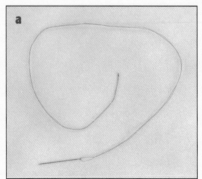
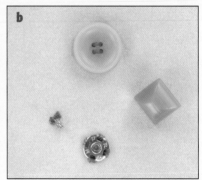

Hand basting temporarily holds fabric together before making your final stitching. Basting may seem like a waste of time, but these hand stitches are much easier to remove than machine stitching. It's also a way to test the fit before you make permanent seams. Running stitches are one of the fastest hand stitches and very easy to remove.

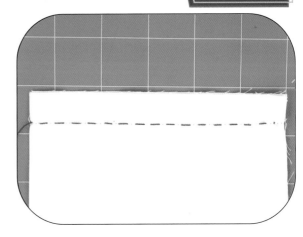

Hand-Baste

① Place the thread knot in the seam allowance so that your machine stitches won't sew over it, making it difficult to remove.

② Place the needle in the seam line that you want to stitch. Bring the needle back up to the right side of the fabric. Repeat until you've basted the desired area.

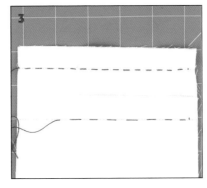
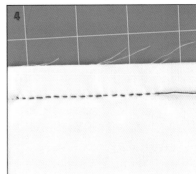

③ Basting stitches are formed by putting the needle in and out of the fabric. They're usually large stitches for easy removal. The length of the stitches will depend on the amount of hold you're looking to achieve.

④ Running stitch is done in the same way that is described for basting, but the stitches are small and uniform. It is used for fine, delicate seam work, where you don't want heavy threadwork to show and gather.

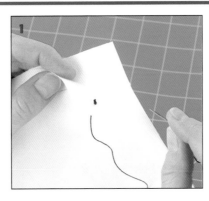
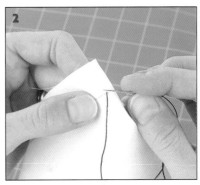

Backstitch

The backstitch is one of the most used hand stitches. It provides a strong seam for mending or construction. By making the stitch with small stitches, you can use it for non-obstructive hand sewing that will show on the outside of a garment. You can also use it to secure the end of hand-sewing stitches.

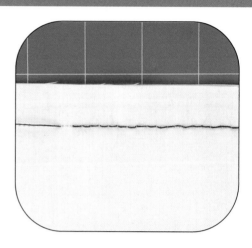

Make a Backstitch

① Secure your thread knot just inside the seam allowance on the wrong side of the fabric.

② Draw the needle straight up through the fabric.

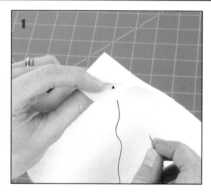
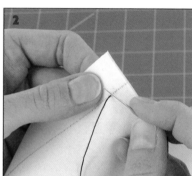

③ Bring the needle down through the fabric *behind* the first stitch, and bring the needle up in front of the thread where you want the next showing stitch.

④ For the second stitch, bring the needle down through the fabric *behind* the stitch butting up against the first stitch. Take a long stitch so that it comes up in front of the thread again. Repeat until you've finished the desired area.

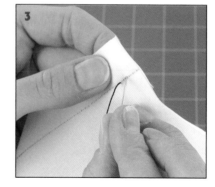
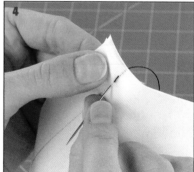

Slipstitch

A slipstitch is used wherever you want the stitches to barely show on the outside of a sewing project. It is a popular hemming stitch and is sometimes referred to as an *uneven catch-stitch*. It's also used to tack down facings (see Chapter 9 for more information). For this example, you'll sew an area of a hem.

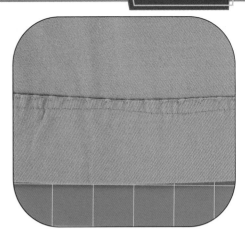

Make a Slipstitch

① Anchor the knot in the finished hem edge.

② Take a tiny stitch in the body of the garment opposite from where your thread came through the hem.

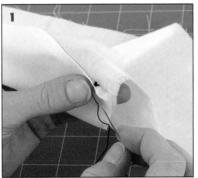

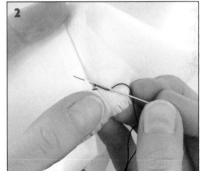

③ Bring the needle back to the hem and sew an approximately ¼-inch stitch; repeat until you're finished. Anchor the end as shown on page 63.

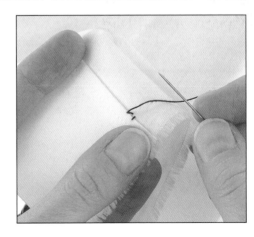

Catch-Stitch

The catch-stitch is a very strong hemming stitch. It's visible on the inside of the garment and is especially suited to hems with a pinked-edge finish, as it holds the pinking down to the garment. Unlike most hand stitches, this stitch is worked from left to right.

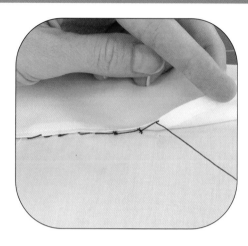

Make a Catch-Stitch

1 Hide the knot inside the hem edge of the garment, bringing the needle to the outside hem edge.

2 Move approximately ¼ inch to the left of where your previous stitch was formed, and make a small stitch that only picks up a few threads of the fabric, inserting the needle from the right to the left.

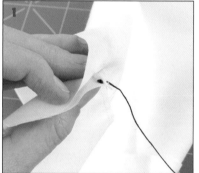

3 Pull the needle through the fabric and make the exact same stitch in the outside of the hem; repeat until you've finished the hem. Anchor the stitching as shown on page 63.

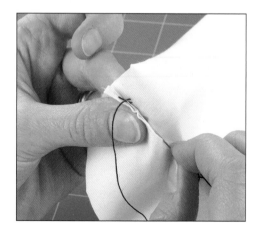

A blind stitch is made with either the catch-stitch or the slipstitch. The stitches are hidden inside the hem and aren't visible unless you pull back the hem to see them. The purpose of a blind hem is to prevent the hem edge from pressing into the outer fabric, which is especially important with bulky fabrics.

The stitches are sewn the exact same way as the slipstitch and catch-stitch described on pages 57 and 58, respectively, except that they're worked inside the hem $\frac{1}{8}$ to $\frac{1}{4}$ inch from the edge of the hem.

Fold the body of the garment back to meet the inside edge of the hem. Do not press the body of the fabric back, just a gentle roll back so that it is possible to keep the hand stitching directly across from the stitches you will be making on the hem.

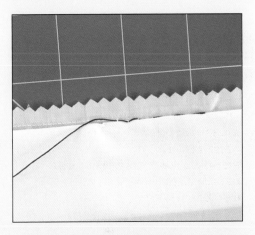

As you stitch, catch just a couple threads of the fabric on the body of the garment and on the hem. Your goal is to have as little stitching as possible show on the inside and outside of the garment while the hand stitching holds the hem in place.

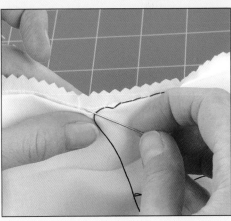

Chain Stitch

A chain stitch is a decorative stitch used for embellishment. It's formed by a series of loops.

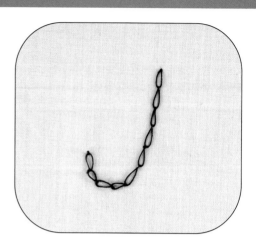

Make a Chain Stitch

①　Fasten the knot on the underside by bringing the needle up from the back side of the fabric. Insert the needle into the fabric right next to where the thread comes up through.

②　Bring the needle back up through the fabric ⅛ to ¼ inch in front of where you went into the fabric. *Do not bring the needle out of the fabric.*

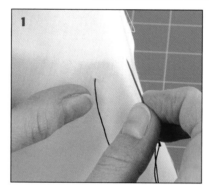
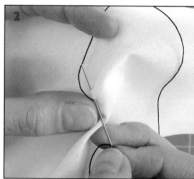

③　Loop the thread over the top side of the needle and down under the point of the needle to the bottom side of the needle to form a loop.

④　Pull the needle up through the fabric and loop. Place the point of the needle into the fabric just inside the top of the formed loop and repeat, making another loop. Repeat until you have the desired amount of chain stitch.

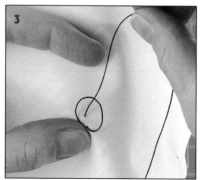
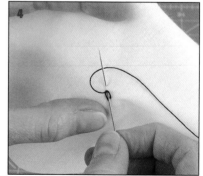

A thread chain is commonly used to create a loop for a button closure. It can also create delicate belt loops and replace the eye of a hook and eye closure. You may notice a small thread chain on lined garments, which loosely holds the lining to the body of the garment.

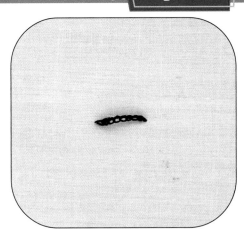

Make a Thread Chain

1 Anchor the knotted thread in the back of the fabric, bringing the needle to the surface. Make one chain stitch where the needle came through the fabric, but hold the loop with your fingers.

2 Pull the needle thread through the loop, creating a new loop.

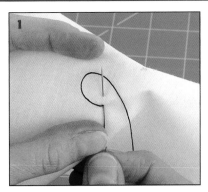

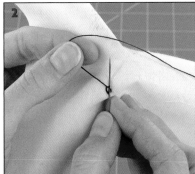

3 Pull the needle and thread through the loop after you've created the desired length of thread chain.

4 Anchor the thread chain in the fabric at the desired position using a backstitch.

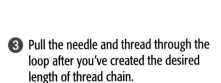

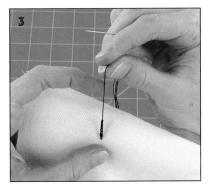

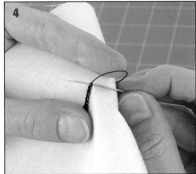

Buttonhole Stitch/ Blanket Stitch

As sewing machines evolved to have built-in buttonhole-making devices and stitches, the hand-sewn buttonhole stitch became a more decorative stitch. The same stitch is often referred to as a *blanket stitch* because it's often used to edge blankets.

Make a Buttonhole/Blanket Stitch

1 Hide the thread knot inside the item you're sewing to the left side of the area you'll be sewing.

2 Insert the needle in the same spot that you hide the knot, and bring it to the edge of the sewing area and though a loop of the sewing thread.

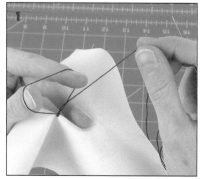
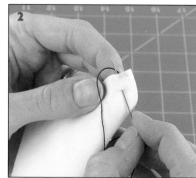

3 Insert the needle ½ inch or a desired distance from the first stitch and repeat, bringing the needle through the loop.

4 To cover the edge of a buttonhole opening, make the exact same stitch, but leave no space between the stitches, so that the entire raw edge is covered.

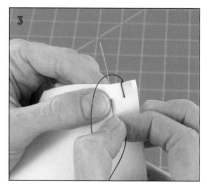

TIP

Polar Fleece fabric requires no seam finishes. A single-cut piece of Polar Fleece is usable as a blanket, but a buttonhole stitch added to the edges sewn with thread or yarn makes a decorative finish.

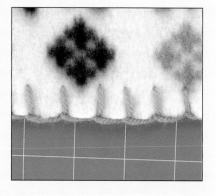

People often complain that their hand sewing always comes undone. If this sounds familiar, the way you end your stitching may be the culprit.

End a Hand Stitch

1 Find a spot that isn't going to show the end of the area you're sewing (the same way you hide the knot when you started sewing). Sew a backstitch and repeat.

2 Move over from the first backstitch location and repeat, creating two backstitches.

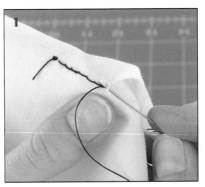
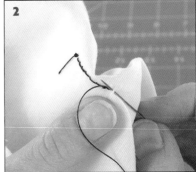

3 In very fine fabrics, where multiple backstitching could leave too much thread, work a chain stitch to make a small knot.

4 Move over and make a second chain-stitch knot.

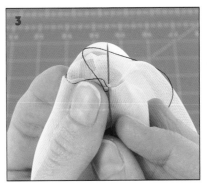
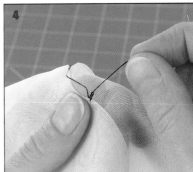

TIP

When you're ending your hand stitching, do not backstitch more than twice on the same spot. Move your ending stitches over just a little so you do not create bulky stitching in one spot.

chapter

6

Basic Techniques

Understanding basic sewing techniques is a stepping stone to bigger and better things. Take the time to master the basics and the more advanced projects will become easy.

The bobbin provides the underside thread for the sewing machine. Properly winding the bobbin is important to achieve the correct tension on the bobbin thread and have an acceptable stitch quality. The best source on how to thread your bobbin is the machine manual. (See Chapter 1 for information on locating a machine manual.)

Thread a Top-Winding Bobbin

1 Most sewing machines wind the bobbin on the top of the machine before it is dropped in or placed in a bobbin case. Place the bobbin on the bobbin winder.

2 Place the thread spool in its position. Guide the thread to the one or two thread guides it must go through on its way to the bobbin.

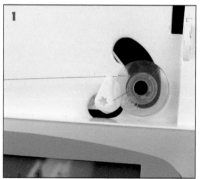
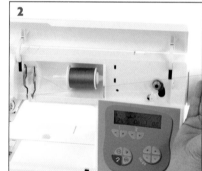

3 Manually wind the end of the thread around the bobbin a few times. If the bobbin has access holes in it, bring the end of the thread through one of the holes and wind it around the bobbin a few times.

4 Gently slide the bobbin holder over toward the bobbin-winding regulator or brake. See close up of bobbin engaged against bobbin-winding regulator in photo at the top of this page.

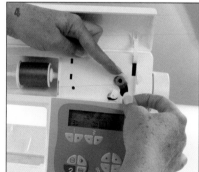

⑤ Hold the end of the hand-wound thread and slowly engage the machine. Allow the machine to partially wind the bobbin, achieving thread covering the entire shaft of the bobbin with two to three layers of thread. Trim the end-tail thread that you've been holding.

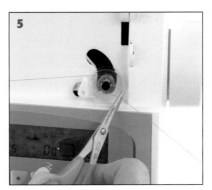

⑥ Keeping the machine speed slow and even, resume winding the bobbin until the sound of the machine changes or the bobbin stops turning because it has filled and is touching the bobbin-winding regulator or brake.

⑦ Slide the bobbin holder shaft and bobbin away from the bobbin-winding regulator or brake.

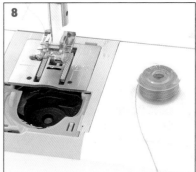

⑧ Place the bobbin in the machine. Leave a long enough tail to thread the bobbin area.

*Note: A small number of sewing machines have bobbins that wind in their final position. These machines with a **bottom-winding bobbin** and usually have a button or latch that must be engaged for the bobbin to wind.*

TIP

Not all bobbins are the same. Even if the size or shape variance is not visible to the naked eye, the wrong size bobbin will affect the operation of your sewing machine or the quality of the stitches. Consult your manual for the correct type of bobbin to use.

Placing the Bobbin in the Machine

Bobbins are inserted in sewing machines in a variety of ways. Your machine manual is the best source for learning the proper way to insert the bobbin.

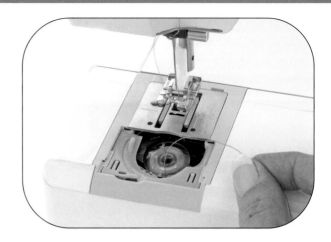

Drop-in Bobbins

Drop-in bobbins do not have a removable bobbin case. The bobbin is set in place. The bobbin tail thread is guided through necessary guides.

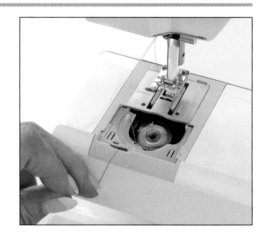

Once the sewing machine is threaded, the needle is lowered (a) and raised by turning the balance wheel to catch the bobbin thread and bring it through the throat plate (b). See pages 70–73 for threading the sewing machinge.

A large variety of sewing machines have a bobbin case. They mount differently from machine to machine. Most have a latch that releases the bobbin case from the machine.

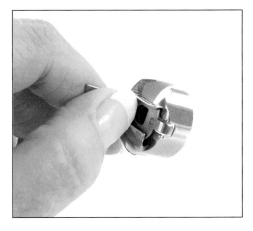

The bobbin tail thread is then threaded though the case slot and tension spring.

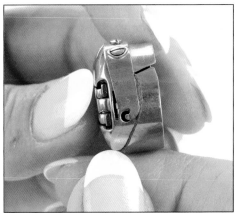

Hold the bobbin case by the latch to insert it back into the machine.

Threading the Sewing Machine

All sewing machines vary slightly in how they're threaded. The best source on how to thread your machine is the machine manual. (See Chapter 1 for information on locating a machine manual.)

Your goal in threading the sewing machine is to get the thread from the spool to the machine needle, through *all* the guides so that the machine will sew well-balanced stitches.

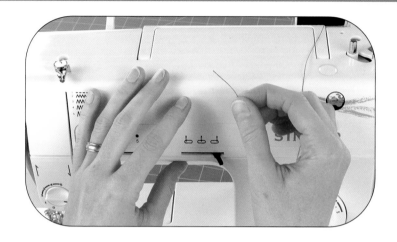

The Threading Diagram

Many older sewing machines have a threading diagram inside the end of the machine.

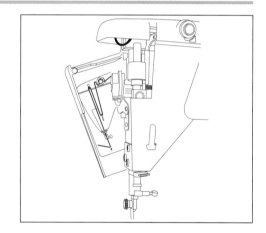

Many new sewing machines have threading diagram arrows on the machine to follow as you thread the machine.

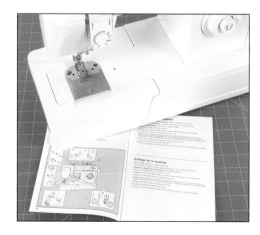

Thread the Sewing Machine

1 Place the machine presser foot up. When the presser foot is down, the tension discs are engaged, and the thread will not sit properly in the tension discs with the foot down.

2 Place the thread on the sewing machine. Thread is held on the spool holder. Spool holders come in assorted varieties. Horizontally built-in spool holders also have a vertical spool holder option. Use the appropriate spool holder for your spool of thread. (See "The Parts of a Sewing Machine" in Chapter 1.)

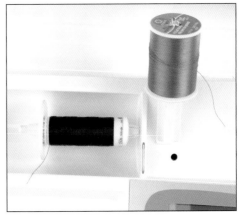

3 Thread guides come in various shapes and forms. The next step is usually a thread guide. It may be a hook design or a button design (a). Drawing thread from the spool, run the thread to the thread guide, which is closest to the spool of thread (b).

CONTINUED ON NEXT PAGE

④ Watch for another thread guide as you move the thread downward to the tension discs. Slide the thread under the tension disc and upward.

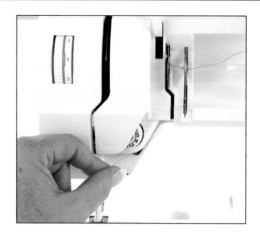

⑤ Guide the thread upward to the take-up lever. The take-up lever may have a slot in it to slide the thread in, or you may have to thread it like a needle eye.

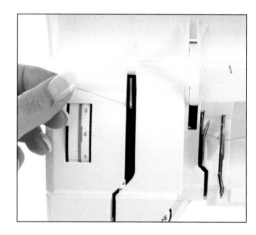

⑥ Once you have the thread through the take-up lever, guide it downward toward the needle. There are usually two thread guides before the thread goes to the needle. One may be on the front of the machine, and one is just under the machine body, almost hidden if you aren't looking for it.

7 Guide the thread to the needle. Just above the needle there is usually a guide you must take the thread through.

8 You made it! You're at the sewing machine needle. Thread the needle, and place the thread tail under the presser foot toward the back of the machine. Thread the bobbin and bring the bobbin thread up through the throat plate.

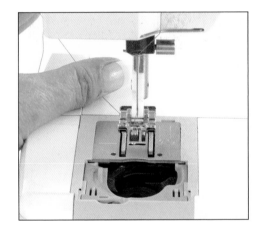

9 Test the stitching on a scrap of fabric.

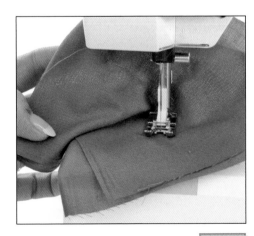

Cutting Fabric with Rotary Cutting Tools

Rotary cutting tools are designed to work together. A rotary cutter will damage the cutting surface if you don't have a rotary cutting mat underneath. These mats are designed to work with only a rotary cutter. Other cutting tools may permanently damage your mat.

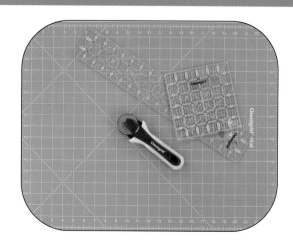

Use Rotary Cutting Tools

1 Place the cutting mat on a hard, flat surface (a). If you use the mat on a soft surface, such as a carpeted floor, the cutter can damage the mat (b).

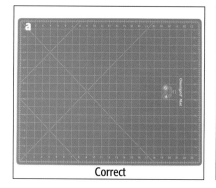

Correct

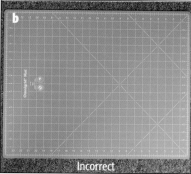

Incorrect

2 Place the fabric on the cutting mat and the ruler on top of the fabric.

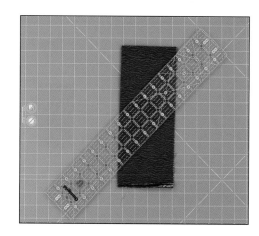

Squares are a basic shape used frequently in quilting as well as other sewing projects. Learning to use a rotary cutting tool and ruler can eliminate accidental parallelograms.

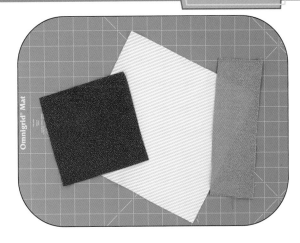

Cut Fabric Squares

1. Starting with well-pressed fabric, line up one line of markings on the ruler with either the selvedge edge or the fold.

2. Place your fingertips on the ruler and apply firm downward pressure to hold the ruler in place. Keep your fingertips away from the ruler's edge.

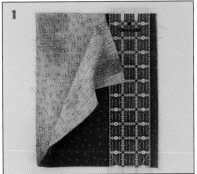

3. Place the rotary cutter blade against the edge of the ruler. Apply firm pressure and slide the cutter along the edge of the ruler. This creates a squared edge.

4. Turn the fabric, so you're using the squared edge on one part of the ruler and use the markings on the ruler to cut to the desired measurements.

Cutting Fabric with Scissors

Sharp scissors are a must. The way you handle scissors affects the way they cut. Specialty scissors have special functions and are built to be used in a specific way. See "Cutting Tools" in Chapter 2 for more information.

Almost all scissors are designed to cut best when they are held at a 45-degree angle to what you're cutting.

Using the proper angle allows you to maintain control of the scissors and obtain accurate cut results. Cutting is one of the first ways you can accidentally change the size of what you are making. Accurate cutting is essential to the results.

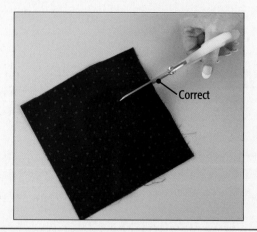

Correct

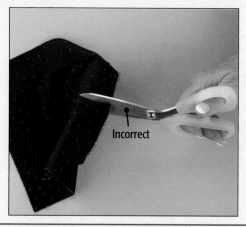

Incorrect

Bent-handle scissors are specifically designed to cut an item on a flat surface so that you don't disturb the layout of what you're cutting. The handle is raised, and the bottom blade glides along the cutting surface.

Appliqué or **duckbill scissors** are designed to not poke into the underlayer of what you're cutting, yet these scissors allow you to cut close to a surface.

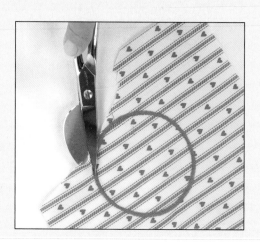

Seam rippers are your best friend to remove stitching. However, you'll want to be very careful to use them correctly so that you don't rip a hole in your fabric as well.

1 From one side or the other of the sewn fabric, gently insert the point of the seam ripper into the middle of a stitch. It should go under the thread and not catch any fabric.

2 Gently tug the seam ripper toward the thread you want to remove until the seam ripper cuts the thread.

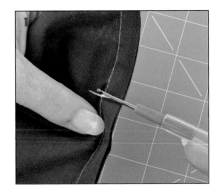

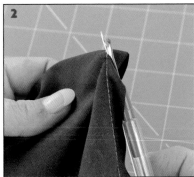

3 Insert the seam ripper in the next stitch the same way and remove that stitch by lifting the thread.

4 If the stitches are loose enough, you may be able to move over a few stitches and gently tug the thread to remove it from the fabric.

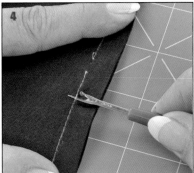

TIP

The best way to ruin your project is to try to work the seam ripper like a snowplow in the middle of the layers of fabric. Before you know what happened, the threads are cut but so is the fabric.

Marking Fabric with Dressmaker's Carbon

Read the package for removal directions on any dressmaker's carbon that you buy. Be sure the removal process is compatible with the fabric you're marking. All markings must be accurate. Keep your markings as small as possible to keep them accurate and prevent removal problems.

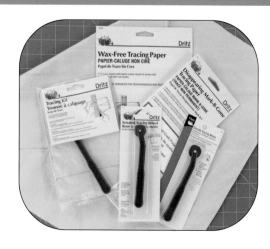

Mark Fabric with Dressmaker's Carbon

1 Fold the paper with the chalk or colored side out.

2 On a hard surface, place the paper so that the marking side of the paper is facing the wrong side of the fabric.

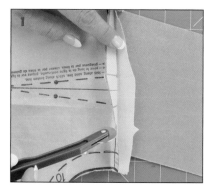
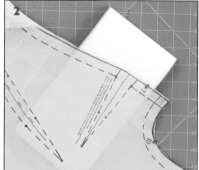

3 Line a straightedge up to the lines you want to transfer and run the tracing wheel along the edge of the straightedge.

4 To transfer dots, cross the straight line to form an *X* at the center of the dot.

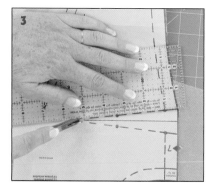
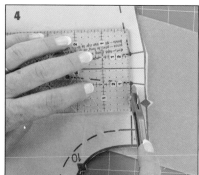

Tailor's chalk and quilting pencils are wonderful tools to make temporary alteration marks when someone has on a garment. They can also be used to transfer pattern markings.

Mark Fabric with Tailor's Chalk and Quilting Pencils

1 Place a straight pin straight through the pattern marking to hold the location that needs to be marked.

2 Gently pull the layers of fabric apart without moving the straight pin.

3 Use a quilting pencil or the corner of the tailor's chalk to mark the fabric where the straight pin is going through the fabric.

Machine Basting

Basting is the process of temporarily joining fabric to test the fit of the fabric pieces or garment. Basting is loose stitches that will be removed once you have sewn the permanent stitches. See also "Hand Basting/Running Stitch" in Chapter 5.

To Machine-Baste

1 Set your sewing machine stitch length on the longest stitch (biggest number) possible.

2 Sew the basting just to the inside edge of where you'll do your permanent stitching, so that it will be removable by not being sewn over with the permanent stitches.

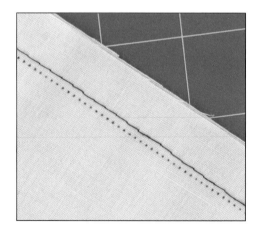

FAQ

Should I secure the end of my basting stitches?

Do not backstitch the end of your basting stitches. It just makes them harder to remove.

Gathering is used to create ruffles. The ruffles may be from fabric, lace, or anything that can be sewn and drawn together. Gathering is also used in many garments to add shape and decorative details.

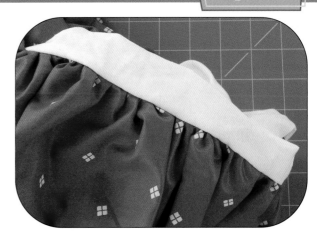

Gathering Fabric

1 The first step to any gather is creating loose stitches that can be pulled without breaking so that the fabric will gather evenly. Sew basting stitches just inside the seam line that will be gathered, leaving a 4- to 5-inch tail of thread.

2 Sew a second row of basting (and sometimes a third row) just inside the seam allowance from the first row of basting. A third row of basting, when the amount of seam allowance allows it, will give you more control to evenly space your gathers.

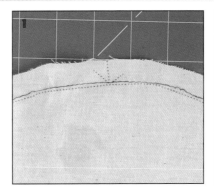

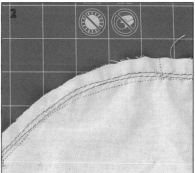

3 Sort the tails of thread so you'll be tugging at just the top threads or just the bobbin threads. If you try to pull the gathers with upper threads *and* bobbin threads, you'll tighten the stitches and the threads will not gather the fabric.

4 Gently start tugging the thread and sliding the fabric up the basting stitches until you have the desired amount of gathering.

Note: *Use good-quality thread! It's very frustrating to have the gathering almost achieved only to have the thread break, forcing you to start over.*

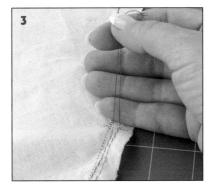

Easing

Easing fabric is the process of making one piece of fabric fit to another without causing any tucks or gathers in the fabric. Easing is usually called for where a rounded piece is going into a straighter piece, such as fitting a sleeve into an armhole.

Ease a Sleeve

1 As with gathering, to begin the easing process, baste two lines of stitches.

2 Pin the sleeve cap to the armhole of the garment at the top and marked dots.

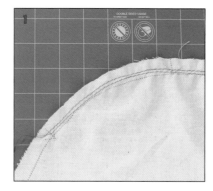

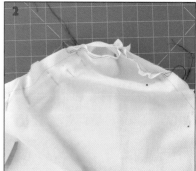

3 To ease in the fullness of the sleeve, gently tug at just the top sewing thread or just the bobbin threads to draw up the fabric without making gathers. Slide the fabric the same way you do when gathering, but don't allow the fabric to bunch.

4 Even out the easing to evenly distribute the fullness and pin the sleeve in place. Sew the eased area. If tucks or gathers occur, remove the stitching and re-ease the fabric.

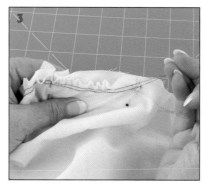

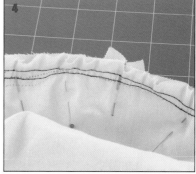

When you sew, you're the designer and the possibilities are endless! Decorative appliqués are one of the many ways to add flair and distinction to anything you make.

Decorative Additions

You can sew badges and purchased appliqués by hand, using small stitches from the back side of the fabric, moving around the edge of the badge or appliqué until the entire edge is sewn down.

If you're confident of your sewing machine skills, you can also machine-sew badges and appliqués in place with matching thread, as close to the edge as possible (a). Badges or appliqués with small borders, which are not likely to curl up, can be machine-sewn just inside the border (b).

Pleats

Pleats are relatively large folds of fabric that are pressed into place. They might be partially or completely stitched in place.

Pleats are usually added as part of a pattern, with the pattern taking into consideration the amount of fabric the pleats will use.

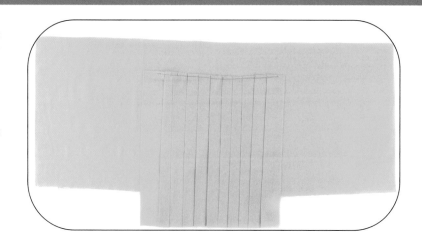

Mark Pleats

Pattern markings for pleats include a fold line and a placement line.

Note: *Use different color markings for each type of line to make the markings easier to follow when you're making the pleats.*

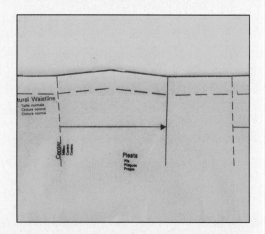

These markings are transferred to your fabric (a) using one of the mark techniques described on pages 78 and 79. The fold line is folded and placed on the placement line (b).

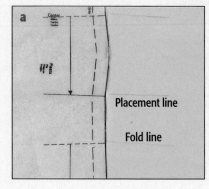

Placement line

Fold line

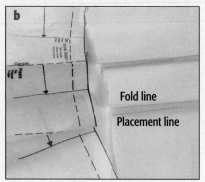

Fold line

Placement line

Types of Pleats

SIDE PLEAT

Side pleats (sometimes called *knife pleats*) have even folds all facing in the same direction. This type of pleat has one fold line marking and one placement line marking.

BOX PLEAT

Box pleats are made with two even folds turned away from each other, with the underside folds meeting each other (a).

INVERTED PLEAT

Inverted pleats are made the same way as box pleats, except that the meeting edges are on the top side (b).

An inverted pleat allows you to add a separate fabric as a decorative element and hide the seaming within the pleat.

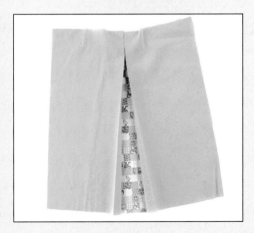

chapter 7

Sewing Seams and Seam Finishes

Seams are fundamental to almost every sewn item. Strong seams are important in garment and craft sewing to extend the life of the garment or item through use and laundering. Imagine the nightmare a weak seam in a pair of slacks could create when you bend over at the super-market. No one wants that to happen!

Seam finishes are important. Although most seam finishes are not seen, they prevent seam allowances from becoming frayed, which could weaken the seam.

SINGER

Seam Guides

Seam guides are built in on the throat plate of most sewing machines, but other options are also available to help create the perfect seam. Learning to watch the seam guide and not the sewing machine needle is the first step in achieving straight, even seams.

Types of Seam Guides

Throat-plate markings are in the most commonly used increments of an inch. Many machines have an optional seam guide that screws on to the bed of the sewing machine. It then slides into position to form a barrier that prevents you from going beyond the set limit (a).

Notions companies have magnetic tools available to set another type of barrier (b).

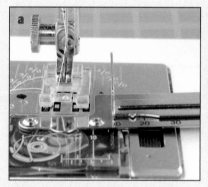

We all have things around the house that can also be used as seam guides. A strip of masking tape is a visible guideline (a).

A stack of sticky notes can be placed on the sewing machine bed to create a raised barrier to prevent going beyond the desired seam allowance (b).

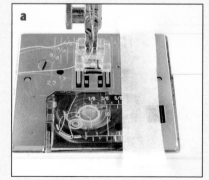

The capability of machines to change needle position also changes the reliability of built-in machine seam guides. Some machines only have European markings.

If your sewing machine doesn't have markings or you just want to be sure the markings are still in sync with the machine needle, there is a very simple way to test the settings.

1 Place a tape measure horizontally under the sewing machine needle. Allow the needle to penetrate the tape measurement for the seam allowance you desire.

2 Place your desired seam guide at the end of the tape measure.

 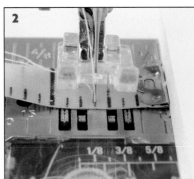

3 A guide as a turning point allows you to keep all topstitching an even distance from the edge of an item (a). Create your own guide so you know when to turn a corner by placing the tape measure vertically (b). Always have the sewing machine needle *all* the way down when you turn a corner to prevent accidentally bending the needle.

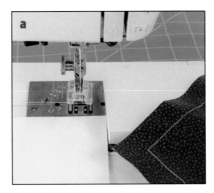 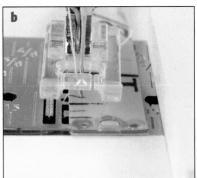

TIP

Seam accuracy is an important part of patterns fitting together and a finished garment fitting the size it was intended to be. Testing the seam allowance settings on your machine is a simple way to be sure you're sewing accurate seams.

Straight Seams

Straight seams usually run with the straight or crosswise grain of the fabric. The seam blends into the fabric when sewn and pressed correctly.

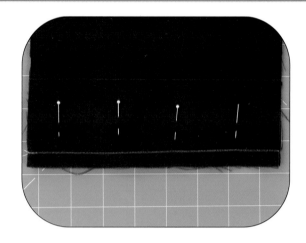

Make a Straight Seam

① Whenever you're going to be sewing the length of straight seam, setting a seam guide is worthwhile unless you're very familiar with your sewing machine.

② Place the beginning of the seam area you want to sew under the presser foot, with a seam allowance of a few stitches behind the needle. The shaft that holds the presser foot is usually this distance from the needle.

③ Reverse-stitch to the end of the fabric. Consult your machine manual to learn how to reverse the stitching on your machine.

④ Sew forward, keeping the edge of the seam allowance as your guide. Sew slowly until you're comfortable.

⑤ When you reach the end of the seam, backstitch (putting the sewing machine in reverse) three or four stitches before raising the presser foot and removing the fabric.

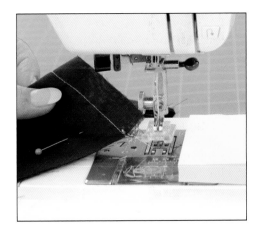

TIP

Accidents happen! If your stitches aren't straight or you wandered so the seam allowance is not consistently even, remove the incorrect stitching.

Sew the correct seam, sewing over three to four stitches at the end of the area you need to correct.

Line up the correct stitching with your sewing machine needle so that you'll be stitching over three or four of the correct stitches.

Curved Seams

Eventually, you'll sew a curved seam. Keeping the curve consistent is the only difference from sewing a straight seam.

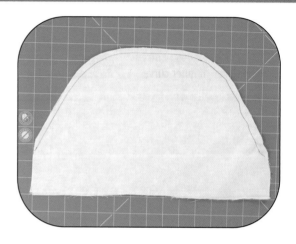

Make a Curved Seam

1. A manufactured seam guide or setting a point as your seam guide is helpful.

2. Backstitch as you would for a straight seam. Sew forward, keeping the seam allowance up against the seam guide as the fabric goes under the needle to stitch the seam.

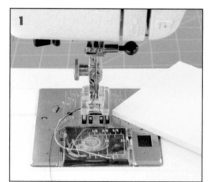

3. A continuously curved seam that ends at the first stitches doesn't have to be backstitched. As the sewing comes back to the first stitch, sew over the top of the first three or four stitches to secure.

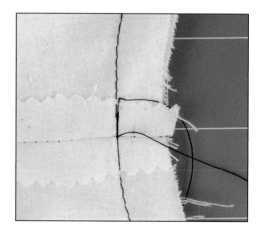

④ Curved seams usually require clipping or notching. It's important to not weaken the seam in the process of clipping the seam. Proper clipping allows the seam to lay flat and eliminates bulk. Clips are small cuts into the seam allowance of inner curves. These clips enable the seam allowance to spread and lay smoothly.

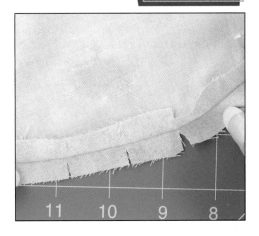

⑤ Notches are cut out of a seam allowance to eliminate bulk on an outer curve so that the seam allowance isn't overlapping when it lays flat.

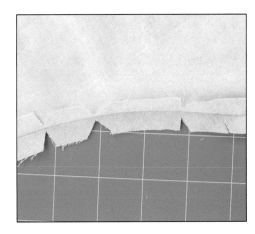

⑥ In some incidences, one seam will need both clipping and notching in order for the seam to lay flat. For example, the front curved seam of a princess-style dress will require clipping and notching in order for the finished seam to press and lay smooth.

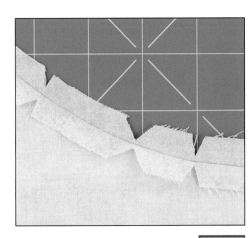

Pressing Seams

Properly pressing a seam can make the difference in the item looking finished or half done. Remember, "pressing" moves the iron up and down, rather than sliding back and forth with the iron, which could distort the unfinished fabric.

Press a Seam

① Press the seam flat the same way that it was sewn. (See photo above.) This helps to set the stitches in the fabric. To create a pressed open seam, open the fabric flat and press the seam open using the tip of the iron.

② Press again from the right side of the fabric.

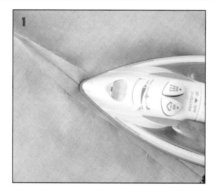

③ To press the seam to one side, first press the seam allowance open. Then press it to one side. Pressing the seam open first allows the seam to lie smoothly.

④ Press again from the right side of the fabric.

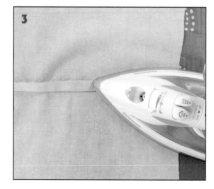
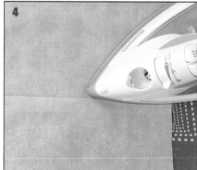

Some fabrics require seam finishing because the fibers will fray and unravel without it. Firmly woven fabrics and Polar Fleece do not need seam finishing, but some fabrics will fray or unravel with tugging and pulling. Medium to loosely woven fabrics may require only a minimal or non-sewn seam finish.

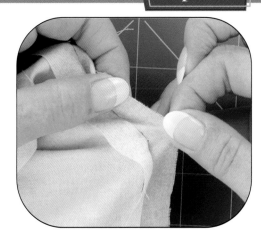

Finish a Seam

If the fabric is tightly woven but you know laundering will cause the fabric to fray, simply pink the edges of the seam allowance (a).

You can also combine the pinking with straight stitching just inside the pinked edge (b).

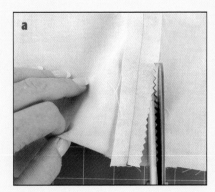
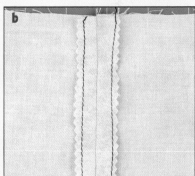

If it won't create bulk that shows through to the outside of the garment when you press the seam, another seam finish can be sewn by turning under ⅛ inch of the seam allowance and sewing the turned edge with a straight stitch (a).

When you sew a lightweight fabric, a seam finish might be unsightly from the finished side. Sew your normal seam and sew it again ⅛ inch into the seam allowance. Trim away the excess seam allowance (b). See also "French Seams" on page 270.

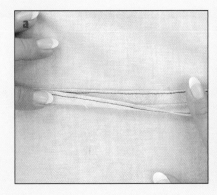
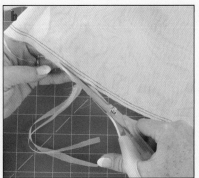

Zigzagged Seam Finishes

One of the easiest seam finishes to sew is a zigzag. It's perfect for medium to heavyweight fabric that tends to unravel or fray.

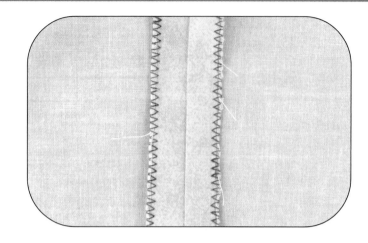

Make a Zigzagged Finish

① Sew the seam and press it as instructed or as you desire.

② With a pressed-open seam, move all the fabric, except the seam allowance you'll be sewing, out of the way.

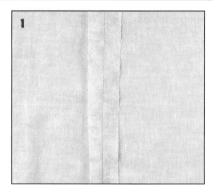

③ Set your sewing machine for a zigzag stitch that's wide enough to enclose approximately one-quarter of the seam allowance. Set the stitch length to a long enough stitch so there isn't a heavy zigzag stitch, but one that will enclose the seam allowance.

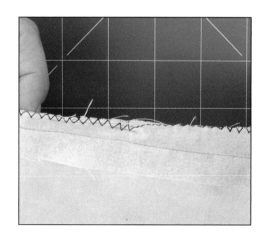

④ Place the seam allowance under the presser foot of your sewing machine with enough fabric behind the needle to allow for backstitching one or two stitches.

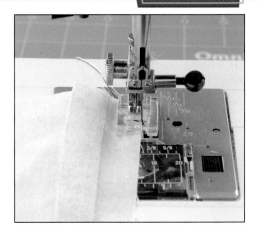

⑤ Backstitch one or two stitches. Sew the zigzag stitch so the right side of the stitch is placing the sewing machine needle just off the raw edge of the seam allowance. Finish the entire seam allowance. Press the seam after you've finished the seam finish.

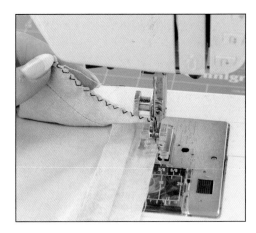

TIP

Some sewing machines have a built-in overcast stitch, which is very similar to a serged stitch. The overcast stitch can be used in the same way as a zigzag stitch.

Corded Seams

Corded seams are used in garments and home-décor sewing. Piping sewn in the seam allowance can add color, dimension, and a decorative touch.

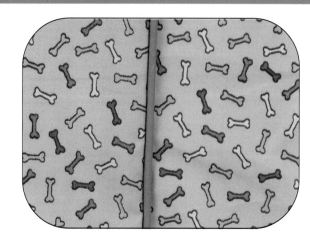

Make a Corded Seam

1. Start with one layer of the fabric that will be forming a seam. Use a zipper foot or cording foot to sew the edge of the raised piping at the seam line. Turn over the fabric.

2. To enclose the piping, place the other layer of fabric that will be making the seam underneath the sewn layer—right sides together.

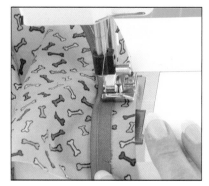

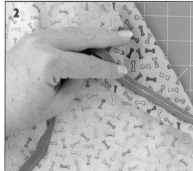

3. Stitch on the original stitching line by using the zipper foot to sew the two pieces of fabric together.

Lace and other decorative touches are often set in the seam line. Collars are a very common area to which lace is added. Lace added to a faced hem adds the illusion of length to a garment.

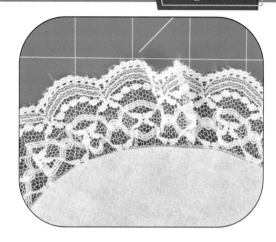

Set Lace in the Seam Line

1 Flat lace can't be added to a curved seam unless you can ease it in to allow for the extension it creates. Flat lace can be added to *straight* seams (a). Gathered lace can be added to any seam allowance (b). Be careful of adding heavy lace to lightweight fabric, as it could weigh down the garment.

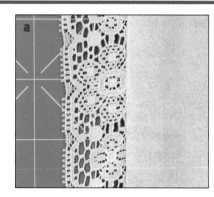
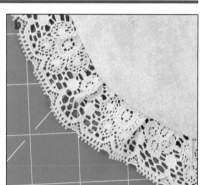

2 Set the lace on the body of the fabric with the gathered edge toward the seam allowance. Position the lace so the gathered edge will be enclosed in the seam allowance. Baste the lace in place.

3 Sandwich the lace between both layers of fabric and sew the seam. Finish the seam as desired.

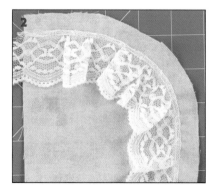

Turning Corners with Seam Insets

Whether you're adding piping, lace, or another decorative addition, turning a corner and having the trim continue as one piece requires a bit of special handling.

For these examples, we're using piping because it's easier to see. Lace and other trims set in the seam would follow the same method.

Turn an Outside Corner

1 Sew the straight edge until you reach where the corner should be turned.

2 With the needle in the fabric, lift the presser foot. Clip the piping seam allowance close to the seam line.

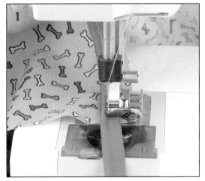

3 Rotate the fabric to set up sewing the other edge of the corner. Align the piping or inset trim to the seam line.

4 Lower the presser foot and continue sewing.

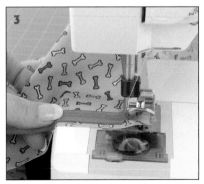

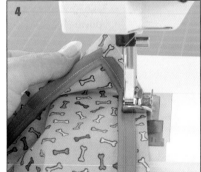

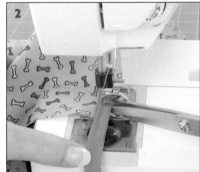

Turn an Inside Corner

1️⃣ Sew the straight areas as described in the preceding section. At the corner with the needle all the way in the fabric and the presser foot up, trim a *V* in the piping or trim seam allowance.

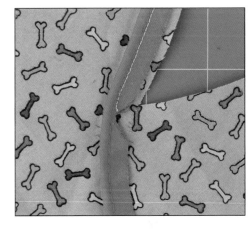

2️⃣ Pivot the corner to set up sewing the other edge of the corner.

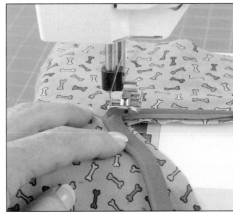

3️⃣ The *V* cut in the piping seam allowance will close up and meet itself. Place the presser foot down and continue sewing.

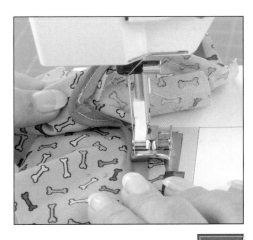

8

Making Darts

Darts are a basic shaping technique, which are commonly found at the bust, back waist, and hips of garments. They transform a flat piece of fabric to one with dimension. A properly sewn dart will blend into the fabric by having a smooth taper to the end of the dart rather than a gap of fabric. The dart allows the garment to fit the body shape.

SINGER

Marking Darts

Transferring pattern marks accurately enables the fabric you're sewing to maintain the intended sizing and ensures that the duplicated darts match on the left and right side of a garment.

As long as the fabric type will allow, dressmaker's carbon is the most accurate way to transfer dart markings.

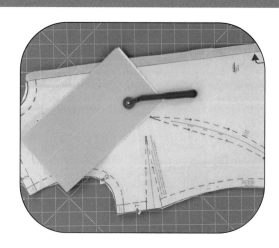

Use Dressmaker's Carbon to Mark Darts

1 If the fabric has been cut with the wrong sides together, place the carbon between the layers of fabric under the dart markings on the pattern.

2 If the fabric has been cut with the right sides together, place the carbon on the outside of the fabric under the dart markings.

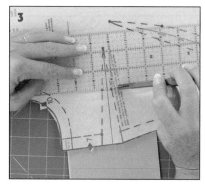

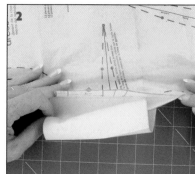

3 Mark the dots that are opposite from each other by placing a straightedge across both dots and marking perpendicular to the stitch lines. Repeat for all the dart dots. Mark at both dots, lifting the tracing wheel between the dots.

4 Place the straightedge along the stitching line and transfer the lines to the fabric.

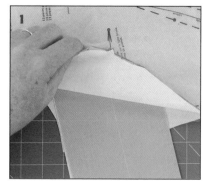

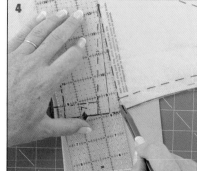

Pinning and Basting Darts

Pinning and basting darts is the only way to ensure accuracy. It might take a few minutes more, but it is much better to pin and sometimes baste than to have to rip out stitches.

Pin and Baste

1. Starting at the widest part of the dart, insert a straight pin in the seam line and dot. Fold the dart to have the straight pin come through the opposite dot. Repeat for all of the dots.

2. Bulky and slippery fabrics may require basting. You should *never* sew over straight pins. If you aren't comfortable with removing pins as you sew, basting is a required step. Basting holds the entire length of the dart in place as you sew it.

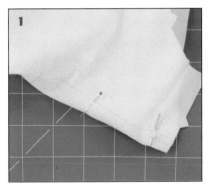

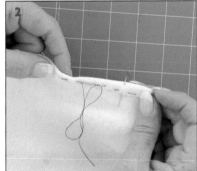

3. Using a hand-sewing needle with a single thread, anchor the knot in the body of the dart so it won't be caught in machine stitching. Insert the needle *just* inside the stitching line, through to the opposite side the same way you inserted with the straight pin.

4. Sew a running stitch in the dart area just inside the stitching line. Anchor the end of the thread outside the stitching line.

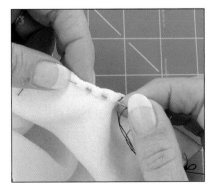

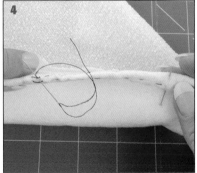

Basic Darts

Darts are not difficult to sew, but they aren't the same as a seam. Never back-stitch the point end of a dart.

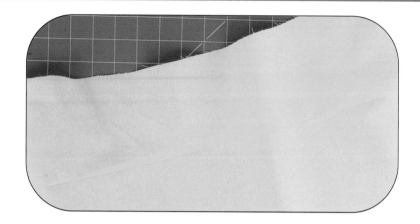

Sew a Dart

1 Starting at the seam line at the widest part of the dart, place the sewing machine needle in the seam line.

2 Put the presser foot down and back-stitch, *if* the wide part of the dart is in a seam line. (See Double-Pointed Dart on page 108.)

 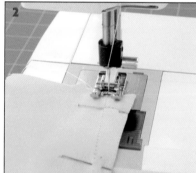

3 Remove straight pins as you approach them with the sewing machine needle.

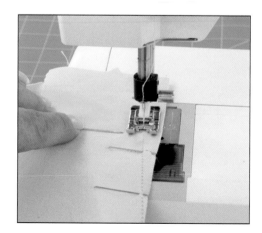

4 Sew the majority of the dart on the marked seam line stopping near the pointed end of the dart. Reduce the stitch length to as short a stitch as possible without puckering the fabric. Sew to the end of the dart within one or two stitches from the edge so the dart comes to a point.

5 Leave a tail of thread as you remove the fabric from the sewing machine.

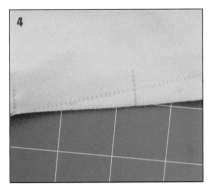
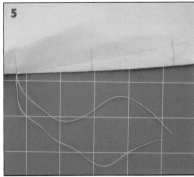

6 Make two square knots in the end of the tail thread. Snug the knots to the end of the machine stitching.

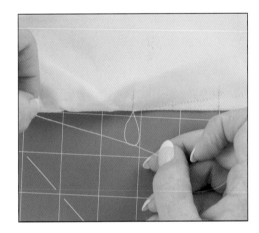

7 Trim the tail threads close to the knots.

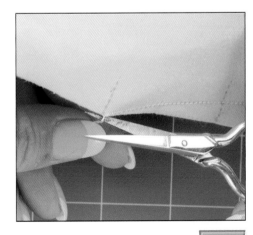

Double-Pointed Darts

Double-pointed darts do not end in a seam line. They draw more fabric in at the middle of the dart with two ends gradually reducing the amount of "taking in" that the dart achieves.

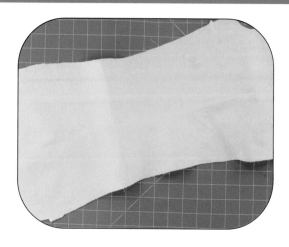

Make the Double-Pointed Dart

1 Double-pointed darts are pinned and basted as any other dart. Sewing double-pointed darts starts at the middle part of the dart. Place the sewing machine needle two or three stitches behind the center of the dart.

2 Sew to the end of the dart and trim tail thread as described in the previous section.

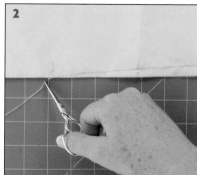

3 Place the center of the dart back under the sewing machine needle to sew the other end of the dart. Place the needle so that you'll be sewing over three to four stitches without backstitching.

4 Sew to the end of the dart and finish sewing the end of the dart. Trim the center tail threads.

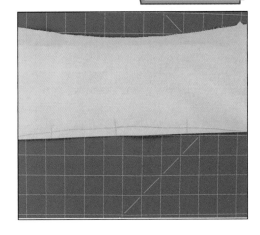

5 Clip the center of the dart so that the fabric will lay flat for pressing.

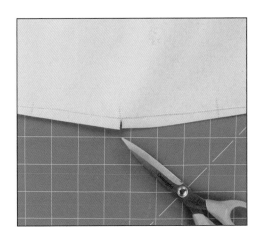

6 Loosely woven fabric is apt to fray through the center of the dart. Reinforce the center of the dart by stitching a second row just inside the original stitching line.

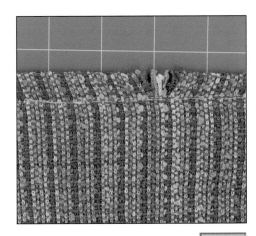

Special Finishes for Darts

Most darts only require pressing well to finish them, but there are a few exceptions.

Curved Darts

1 Curved darts have curved stitching lines. The curve enables the dart to take the most fabric in at a location other than the end or middle of the dart. They're sewn as any other dart. Because they aren't a straight dart and will not lay smoothly if left as sewn, you must trim the body of the dart to ⅝ inch.

2 Sew a second line of stitching just inside the first line of stitching. End the dart before the point so you don't create a bulky point.

3 Clip at curves, without clipping the stitch line, to allow the dart to be pressed flat to the body of the garment.

Bulky and Wide Darts

1 Bulky and wide darts are likely to show through or leave pressing lines if they aren't trimmed. Trim the body of the dart to within ½ inch to 1 inch from the point.

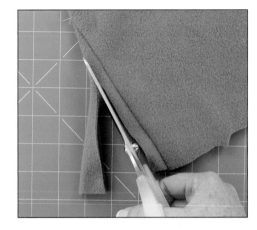

2 After properly pressing the dart, this type of dart is pressed open and the point flattened.

TIP

Keep the darts in mind when choosing your fabric. Many bulky fabrics are also very loosely woven. Do not attempt to add a seam finish to the trimmed dart. Stitch just inside the original stitching and line the garment if necessary to protect the trimmed dart.

Pressing Darts

Pressing as you sew achieves a finished, tailored appearance as well as smooth areas to join seams.

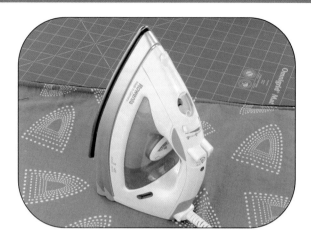

Standard Dart Pressing

1. Press the dart as it was sewn. *Do not press beyond the point of the dart,* because it will create a crease beyond the dart.

2. Open the garment.

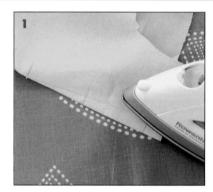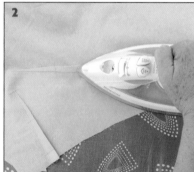

3. Use a pressing ham, the end of the ironing board, a sleeve board, or even tightly rolled towels to ensure that your final pressing maintains the shape that was added to the garment by the dart.

Directional Dart Pressing

1 Vertical darts are pressed to the center of the fabric piece or garment unless instructed differently in the pattern directions.

2 Horizontal darts are pressed downward unless instructed differently in the pattern directions.

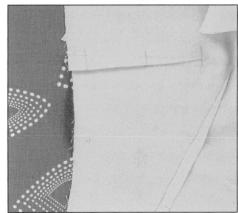

TIP

A press cloth is a handy tool to use when pressing a dart. You prevent adding a sheen to your fabric from pressing and are able to thoroughly press the dart for a professional appearance.

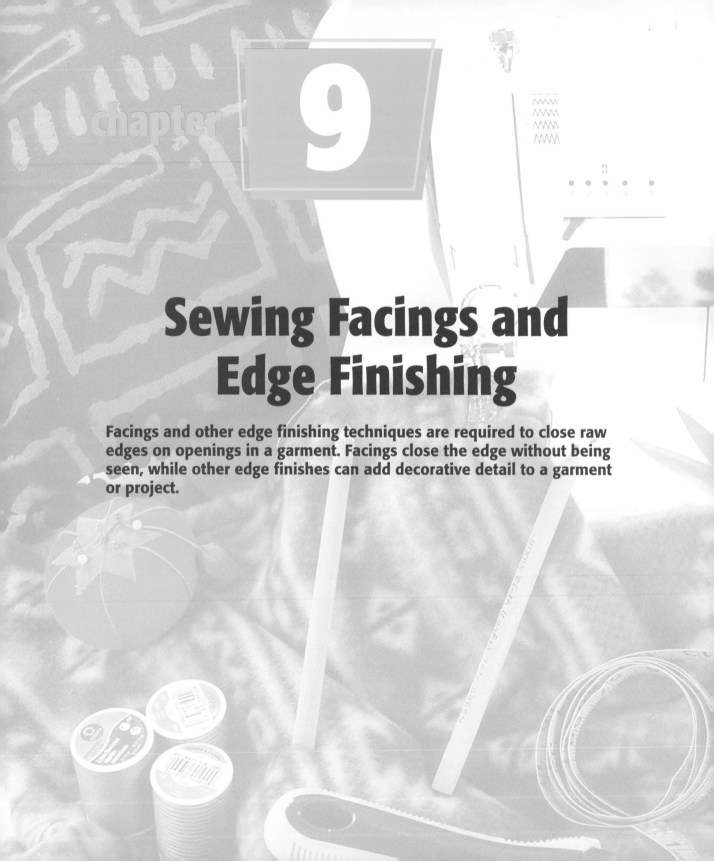

chapter 9

Sewing Facings and Edge Finishing

Facings and other edge finishing techniques are required to close raw edges on openings in a garment. Facings close the edge without being seen, while other edge finishes can add decorative detail to a garment or project.

SINGER

Preparing a Facing

A facing piece needs a small amount of preparation on its own before you can join it to the other parts of the garment.

Prepare a Facing

① Transfer pattern markings as you would for other pattern pieces.

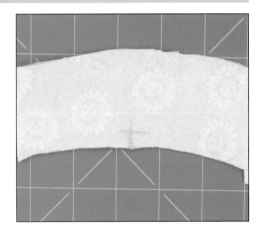

② Stay-stitch and interface the facing pieces. Interfacing will help the facing stay inside the garment as well as add shape to the area of the garment. (See more on Interfacing in Chapter 4.) Stay-stitching is a line of stitching on a single layer of fabric, just inside the seam line, which stabilizes off-grain edges of fabric. It prevents the fabric from becoming distorted and stretching as you work the piece.

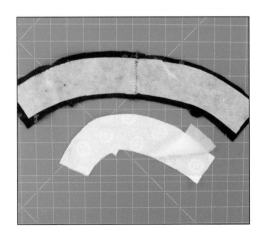

3 Proceed with the pattern directions for joining the facings.

Note: Not all patterns follow the same procedure for joining facing pieces. The method shown here is one of many.

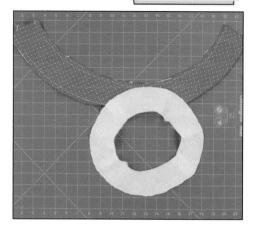

4 Finish the edge of the facing that is not attached to the garment. The finish on the edge of the facing will depend on the weight of your fabric. Use a finish that is similar to the seam finish that you're using in the rest of the garment.

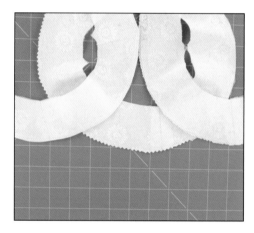

5 On cotton-weight fabrics, the facing is usually finished by stitching ¼ inch from the raw edge, pressing the raw edge to the wrong side of the facing along the stitching line, and stitching.

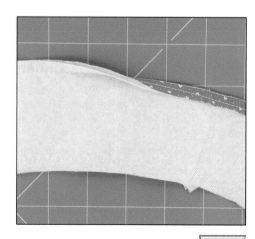

Grading and Clipping a Facing Seam Allowance

Most patterns will tell you to trim and clip the seam allowance. Grading the seam allowance reduces bulk and helps the facing to stay inside of the garment. No one is actually going to grade you on how you trim the seam allowance, but once you learn to grade a seam, you'll be giving yourself an A+ for how well the facing lies.

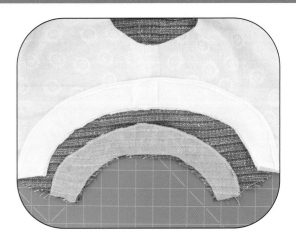

Clip a Seam Allowance

1 Once you've sewn the facing to the body of the garment, trim the seam allowance in half.

2 Trim the facing seam allowance in half again so that it's shorter than the garment seam allowance.

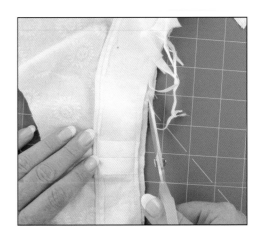

3 Clipping a facing seam allowance enables the facing to fit smoothly when you press the entire area flat. Clipping is done at any curved area. Clip toward the seam allowance without cutting any stitches.

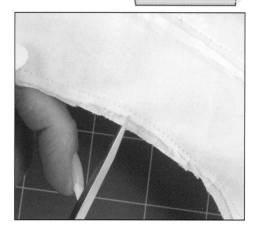

4 Clipping loosely woven fabric may cause the seam to weaken and even fray into the part of the garment that will show. This can be avoided by clipping one layer of the seam allowance at a time. Move the scissors so that the clip on each layer is close to the other layer's clip but not at the exact same location.

TIP

Always take the time to press the seam and then press the seam allowance to the facing side. You'll achieve a professional result if you press as you go.

Under-stitching, sometimes called *stitch-in-the-ditch*, makes all the difference in keeping a facing inside the garment and presenting a smooth edge on the finished garment without the facing showing.

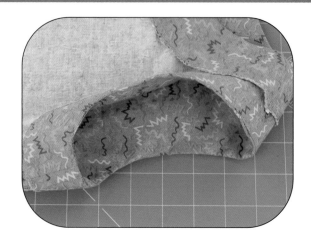

1 Press the graded seam allowance toward the facing. Press both sides of the facing to be sure you have a smooth edge.

2 Place the facing under the needle of the sewing machine, right side up, with the seam allowance staying toward the facing.

3 Your goal is to stitch as close to the seam as possible without actually sewing in the seam line. Use an inside edge of your presser foot as a sewing machine guide to align the needle so it will penetrate the fabric on the facing side of the seam.

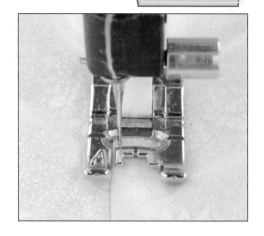

4 Many sewing machines have a way for you to change the needle position to move from left to right. This is a perfect opportunity to use that feature.

TIP

Under-stitching or stitching-in-the-ditch isn't always called for in many places that it can be applied to achieve a finished edge. As your skill expands and you experiment, don't be afraid to add under-stitching to help pieces of fabric lie the way you want them to. When in doubt, use scraps of fabric and test your ideas.

Exploring Bias Tape

Bias tape is used in many home decorating projects as well as some garments. It is a great way to add color and contrast as well as being a sturdy edge.

Types of Bias Tape

BIAS TAPE

Bias tape can be purchased in a variety of widths and forms. You can buy bias tape already pressed and ready to sew, or you can make your own using bias-cut fabric. Tools are available to make the jobs easier. Bias tape is readily available in widths from ¼ inch to 1 inch.

DOUBLE-FOLD BIAS TAPE

Double-fold bias tape is used to cover and bind edges, as a facing, to make ties, and to add decorative accents.

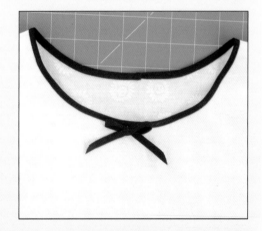

Double-fold bias tape is cut on the bias, the edges are pressed in toward the middle, and then it's pressed in half slightly off center. One side of the tape is narrower than the other so that both edges are easily caught in the stitching when sewing (a).

The narrow side is always on the top sewing side so that the wide edge is under the fabric and will be caught in the stitching (b).

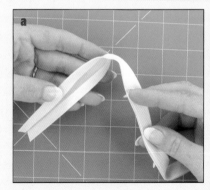

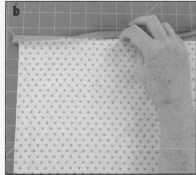

SINGLE-FOLD BIAS TAPE

Single-fold bias tape is made with fabric that is cut on the bias and the raw edges are folded in.

Single-fold bias tape is commonly used to make facings, casing, and as a decorative accent.

All edges of single-fold bias tape are sewn down, usually by topstitching.

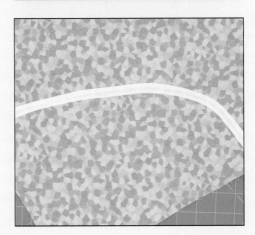

Double-Fold Bias Tape to Enclose Edges

Double-fold bias tape is perfect for enclosing edges and can be used to finish areas such as necklines and armholes.

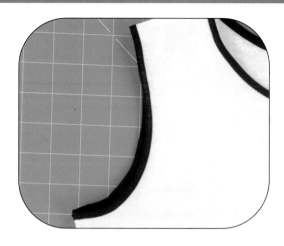

Enclose Edges

1. Trim away the seam allowance where you are going to use bias tape to enclose the edge. Remember that patterns are cut *with* a seam allowance. You have to trim away the seam allowance to enclose the "true" seam line with bias tape.

2. Start at the seam (such as the underarm seam of the garment or the opening edge of a neckline). Always extend the starting point ¼ to ½ inch to have a piece to turn under or enclose with the other end of the bias tape.

3. As an *optional step,* you may want to hand-baste the bias tape to the edge, aligning the fold of the bias tape with the seam line on the fabric. Keep the basting stitches away from the edge of the bias tape to prevent it from being caught in the final sewing.

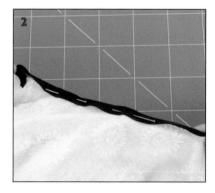

④ On an unending area such as an armhole, follow all the way around the opening keeping the center fold of the bias tape aligned with the seam line until you meet where you started.

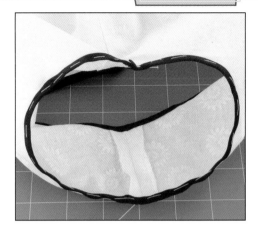

⑤ Fold the end of the bias tape under on itself to match the seam line and enclose the start of the bias tape.

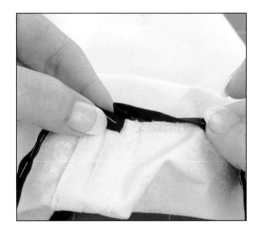

⑥ On an area such as a neckline, follow the same directions, trimming away the seam line and keeping the center fold to the seam line edge. Fold under the ends of the bias tape on itself to form a clean end, even with the fabric edge. Slipstitch the newly made fold to prevent the ends from working their way out. Machine sew the bias tape on top so the wider edge will be caught in the stitching.

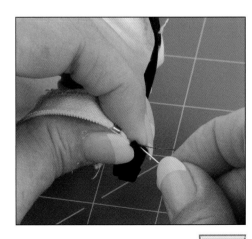

Making Facings with Bias Tape

Use single-fold bias tape for a facing that is not seen on the outside of the garment. This type of facing is commonly topstitched in place but can also be slipstitched for a less visible effect.

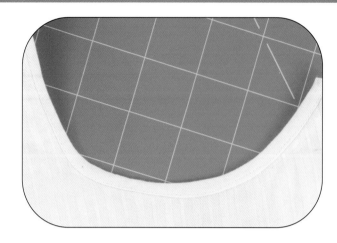

Make Facings

① Place the right side of the bias tape on the right side of the fabric. Align the fold of the bias tape with the seam line. Trim away the excess seam allowance.

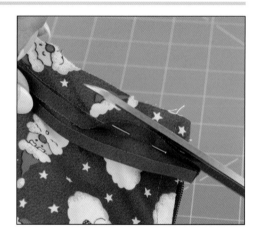

② Stitch the bias tape to the garment along the seam line in the fold of the bias tape.

③ Fold the bias tape up and over the fabric raw edge to the wrong side of the fabric. Slipstitch or topstitch the un-sewn edge of the bias tape.

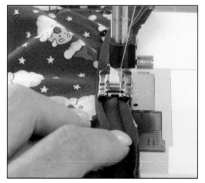

Because bias tape is a versatile edging, sometimes you must turn a corner. A smooth, inconspicuous turn is your goal.

Turn Corners

1 Sew the beginning of the bias tape, stopping at the corner with the machine needle down.

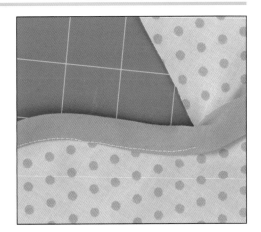

2 Fold the top of the bias tape back on itself and down again to form the corner.

3 Pivot the fabric while holding the corner in place. Place the presser foot down and continue stitching.

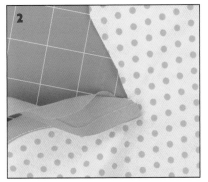

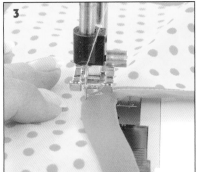

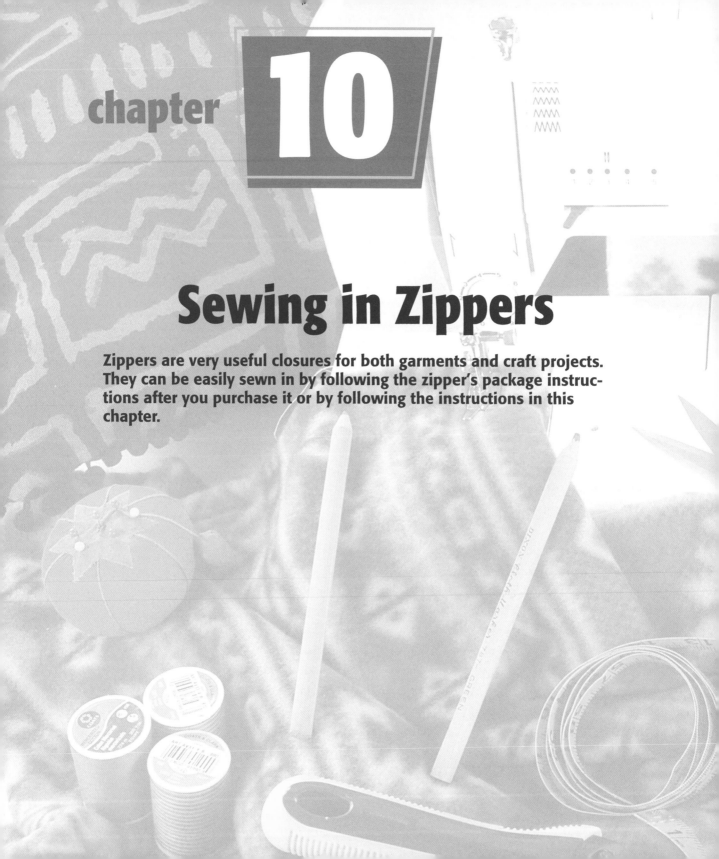

chapter 10

Sewing in Zippers

Zippers are very useful closures for both garments and craft projects. They can be easily sewn in by following the zipper's package instructions after you purchase it or by following the instructions in this chapter.

A zipper provides a secure, smooth closure that eliminates gaps. There are many types of zippers available. The weight of the zipper and the materials it is made of, all play into choosing the zipper you will add to your sewn item.

1. TEETH

The teeth lock together and come apart when the zipper is zipped and unzipped.

2. TAPE

The teeth are attached to the tape, which provides fabric to sew the zipper into a project. Looking closely at the tape, you will notice that most have a variation in the threads of the tape, which serve as a stitching guide as you sew the zipper.

3. SLIDER

The slider has grooves, which fit the teeth of the zipper.

4. PULL

The pull is used to open and close the zipper. Its size corresponds with the size of zipper teeth. A heavy jacket zipper will have a larger pull than an all-purpose dress type zipper. Decorative pulls are available to extend a zipper pull for decorative purposes as well as making it easier for someone who has difficulty grasping a small item.

5. STOPS

Stops are an essential part of the zipper to prevent the slide from going beyond the zipper teeth and for holding non-separating zippers together. The stops are at the top and bottom of the zipper. When you shorten a zipper you create a stop with a bar tack at the bottom of the zipper (see page 272).

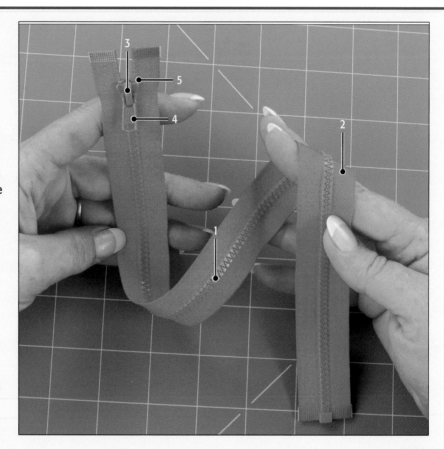

ZIPPER TEETH

There are three types of zipper teeth: polyester coil, molded polyester, and metal. Each type comes in a variety of weights. The thinner or smaller the teeth are, the more delicate the zipper.

THICKNESS AND DURABILITY

The thickness and durability of the teeth you choose will depend on the fabric you're sewing. Thin fabric requires thin zippers. Heavy fabric can carry the weight of large zipper teeth.

COLORS

Choose the color of the zipper the same way you match thread to your sewing project. If a perfect color match is not available, opt for a slightly darker zipper over a slightly lighter zipper.

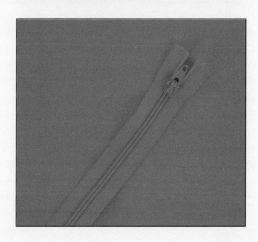

Types of Zippers

An all-purpose zipper is the most common and is available in most places that sell fabric or notions.

Choose a Zipper

ALL-PURPOSE ZIPPERS

All purpose zippers are lightweight zippers with metal teeth or polyester coil teeth (a). All-purpose zippers are usually used in garment construction. They are not bulky, making them a good choice for a dress back (b) or side seam zipper. This type of zipper is closed at the bottom and does not separate. They come in a variety of lengths.

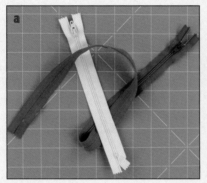

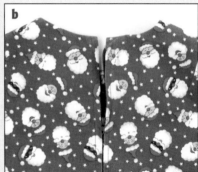

JACKET ZIPPERS

Jacket zippers are separating zippers. They're available in a variety of weights; the weight you choose will depend on the item the zipper is going to be sewn into. A lightweight fleece is apt to sag from the weight of a heavy metal separating zipper. Molded polyester teeth do not weigh as much as metal teeth and won't "weight down" the fabric or cause the garment to sag.

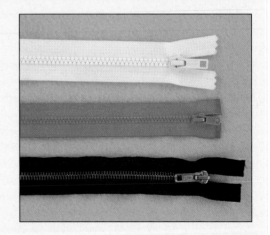

JEAN ZIPPERS

Jean zippers have heavy, strong teeth and are non-separating. They have a strong, durable, low-profile slider so the fabric over the zipper will lie flat. The slider also has a durable lock to prevent the slide from sliding down unless you want to open the zipper. Jean zippers match the construction and durability of jeans.

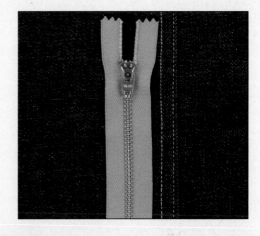

INVISIBLE ZIPPERS

Invisible zippers have polyester coils for teeth. They're lightweight, fine zippers. The way the coils are positioned on the tape allows the coils to hide in a seam. A specialized zipper foot is needed to sew invisible zippers. The instructions for insertion are included with the foot and with the zippers (a).

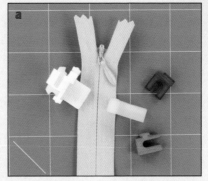

The invisible zipper foot replaces the entire presser foot. Unlike other zipper applications, an invisible zipper is sewn to the fabric before any other part of the seam is sewn (b).

SPECIALTY ZIPPERS

Coveralls, sleeping bags, and upholstery are a few of the things that will require specialty zippers. Specialty zippers can be found at some fabric stores. Almost anywhere that sells zippers will be able to special-order a zipper to meet your needs. Ask the manager of the store for assistance if you can't find the type or length of zipper you're looking for.

Centered Zipper

Centered zippers are usually the first zipper people sew. Taking the time to baste and pressing the seam are the keys to success.

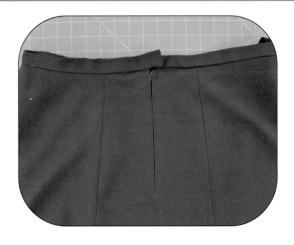

Insert a Centered Zipper

1 Create a normal seam with a normal stitch length until you reach the mark for your zipper. At this mark, stop, backstitch, and change the machine stitch length to a long basting stitch.

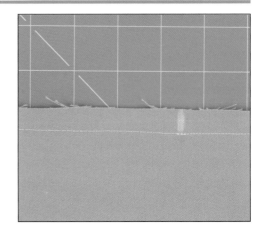

2 Apply seam finishes before inserting a zipper.

3 Press the seam flat as sewn and then press it open, using the tip of the iron to get all the way inside the seam allowance.

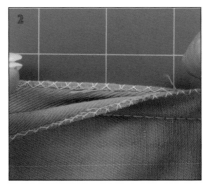

④ Press from the right side of the fabric.

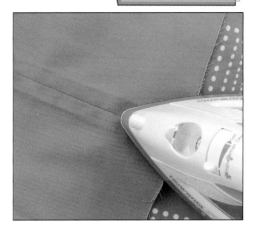

⑤ Open the zipper. With the pull side of the zipper on the seam, align the top of the zipper tape with the top of the seam. Hand-baste the zipper tape to the seam allowance, keeping the edge of the zipper teeth aligned with the seam line. Continue to hand-baste until you reach the end of the zipper.

⑥ Close the zipper. Place the zipper pull up toward the end of the seam. Keeping the zipper flat to the seam, hand-baste the opposite edge.

CONTINUED ON NEXT PAGE

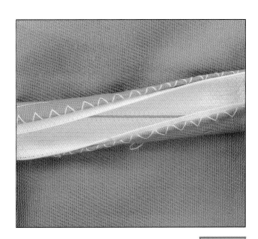

7 With a zipper foot on your sewing machine, place the fabric right side down on the bed of the sewing machine.

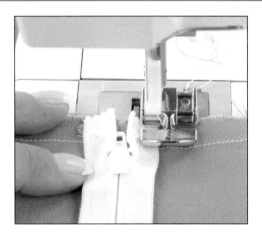

8 Stitch the zipper in place following the stitching guide in the weave of the zipper tape.

9 Continue sewing to the end of the zipper teeth. Stop sewing with the needle down (a). Raise the presser foot and pivot the fabric to sew across the end of the zipper (b). *Be sure to keep the fabric and zipper flat.*

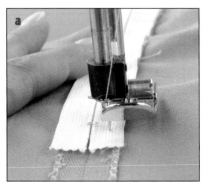

⑩ Pivot again at the stitching guide on the opposite edge of the zipper tape. Continue sewing the second side of the zipper.

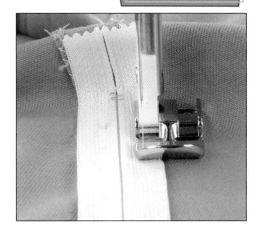

⑪ Check your stitching to be sure that it's an even distance from the seam line on the right side. If it isn't straight and even, remove the zipper stitching and try again.

⑫ When you're satisfied with the stitching on the right side of the fabric, carefully remove the hand basting and the machine basting that is holding the seam closed. Press the finished zipper.

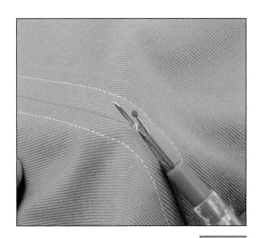

Lapped Zipper

A lapped zipper has only one row of stitching showing on the outside of the garment, with the seam fabric forming a lap to conceal the zipper.

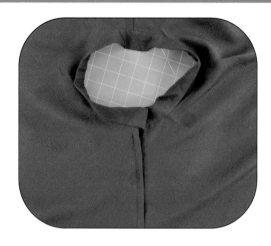

Insert a Lapped Zipper

① Create a seam with a normal stitch length until you reach the mark for the bottom of your zipper. At this mark, stop, backstitch, and change the machine stitch length to a long basting stitch.

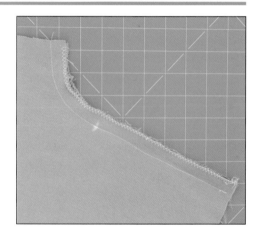

② Press the seam open and apply seam finishes. Place the fabric wrong side up with the bottom area of the zipper placement away from you. Place the body of the fabric under the right side seam allowance. With the zipper closed, place the zipper pull side down on the right side seam allowance, aligning the bottom of the zipper mark and the left side of the zipper teeth to the seam line.

③ Use the zipper foot and sew the zipper tape to the seam allowance.

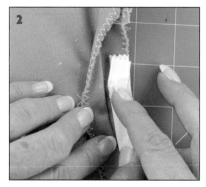

4 Fold the sewn edge under so the pull
side of the zipper is facing up. Press the
seam that attached the zipper tape to the
seam allowance.

5 Stitch the pressed edge of the fabric to
the zipper tape using the opposite side of
the zipper foot.

6 Spread the garment out flat and bring
the zipper over the right side seam
allowance. This will form a small pleat in
the seam allowance.

7 Stitch the zipper, starting at the bottom,
across the tapes and pleats to the guide
line on the zipper tape.

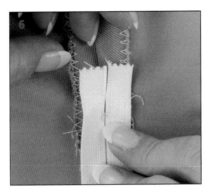 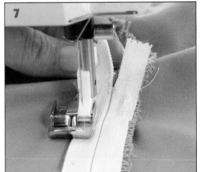

8 Pivot and stitch to the top of the
zipper (a). Remove basting and press (b).

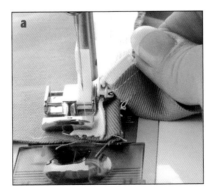 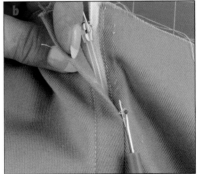

Finishing the Ends of a Zipper

The ends of a zipper in a garment usually end at a neckline with facings or a waistband.

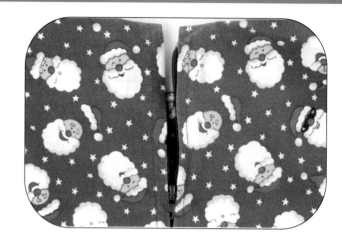

Zipper Finishes

1 When the zipper ends at a facing, after the facing is sewn in place, turn under the ends of the facing at an angle to enclose the zipper tape.

2 Press the turning line of the facing. Trim away any excess bulk from the turned facing.

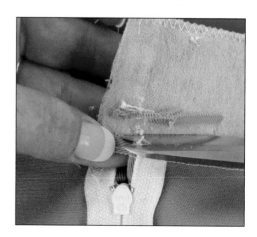

③ Slipstitch the turned edge of the facing to the zipper tape.

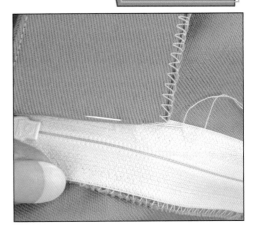

④ When the end of a zipper is enclosed in a waistband, sew on the waistband as written in the pattern instructions.

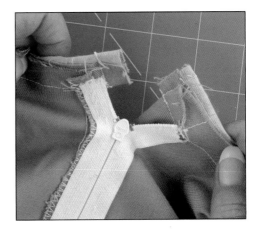

⑤ Trim away extra bulk in the waistband and zipper tape. Finish the waistband as written in the pattern instructions.

chapter 11

Adding Fasteners

Fasteners are a part of the garment that you want to be reliable and strong. Some fasteners are discreet and unseen while others add a decorative touch to a garment or home decorating project. The size and weight of what you choose to close with will depend on the fabric of the item and the amount of pull the fastener will have to endure. Some fasteners can be sewn to the fabric with the sewing machine, some require special sewing machine feet but most are sewn on by hand.

SINGER

Buttonholes

Buttonholes and buttons are among the most common fasteners. The types of buttonholes and the buttons you choose make a difference in the final look of the garment.

BASIC BUTTONHOLE

A sewing machine with a zigzag stitch option has the capability of making a buttonhole. The procedure will vary by machine, and your machine manual will provide detailed instructions. Always test the buttonhole procedure on a scrap of fabric.

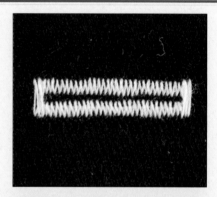

BUTTONHOLES ON STRETCH FABRIC

A buttonhole sewn on stretch fabric should have the stitch length lengthened to allow the fabric to stretch.

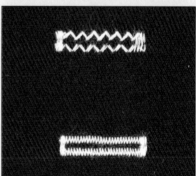

BUTTONHOLE FOOT

Newer sewing machines have a buttonhole foot that can adjust to the length of the button and will automatically sew the buttonhole to fit. They also have a variety of buttonhole types to choose from.

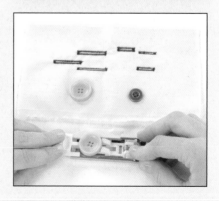

Patterns come with marking for buttonhole and button placement.

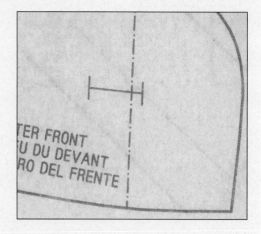

Pattern markings are set for the size button that is called for in the notions section on the envelope.

MISSES' SHIRT: Loose fitting, button front shirt has dropped shoulders, shirt-tail hem, neckband and optional pointed collar. A and C are tunic length. B and D are below waist length. A and B have long sleeves pleated to buttoned cuffs. C and D have short sleeves.

Fabrics: Cotton and Cotton Blends such as Flannel, Gingham, Laundered Cottons, Broadcloth, Chambray, Damask, Lightweight Denim, Sateen, Seersucker. Silks and Silk Types such as Challis, Crepe, Crepe De Chine, Laundered Silks-Rayons, Lightweight Faille. Not suitable for obvious diagonals. Extra fabric needed to match plaids, stripes or one-way design fabrics. For pile, shaded or one-way design fabrics, use with nap yardages/layouts.

Notions: Thread, ⅛" molded shoulder pads (opt.). **A:** Nine ½" buttons. **B:** Eight ½" buttons. **C:** Seven ½" buttons. **D:** Six ½" buttons. Look for Simplicity notions.

BODY MEASUREMENTS										
Bust	30½	31½	32½	34	36	38	40	42	44	In
Waist	23	24	25	26½	28	30	32	34	37	"
Hip-9" below waist	32½	33½	34½	36	38	40	42	44	46	"
Back-neck to waist	15½	15¾	16	16¼	16½	16¾	17	17¼	17¾	"
Sizes	6	8	10	12	14	16	18	20	22	
Sizes-European	32	34	36	38	40	42	44	46	48	

If you use a different button size than is listed on the pattern, you will have to adjust the length of the buttonhole. The length of the buttonhole opening should equal the width of the button plus the height (a).

Always test your buttonhole and button combination on a scrap of fabric before sewing them on your project. Slit the test buttonhole open and test that the desired button will fit through the opening (b).

Note: *If the buttonhole starts to pucker, use stabilizer under the buttonhole.*

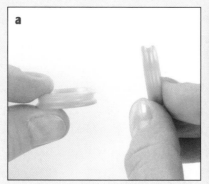

Flat Buttons

Flat buttons are the most frequently used buttons. They're available in a variety of colors and made from a variety of materials. Some sewing machines are capable of sewing on buttons. Refer to your machine manual to see how it is done.

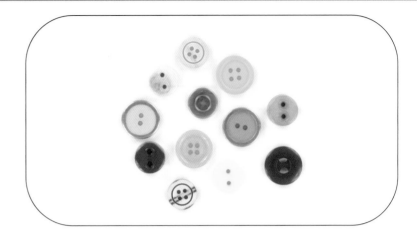

Sew on a Flat Button

1 Flat buttons have two or four holes. Thread a hand-sewing needle with a double thread to match the button. Have a toothpick or thick needle at hand.

2 To mark the placement of the button, overlap the buttonhole on the fabric where the button will be placed. Then place the button on the buttonhole. Place a pin through the button and buttonhole. Gently lift the buttonhole layer and mark the button area (on the fabric) at the straight pin.

3 Anchor the hand-sewing thread on the wrong side of the fabric by making two to three stitches at the center mark of the button placement (a).

4 Bring the needle up through a hole in the button (b).

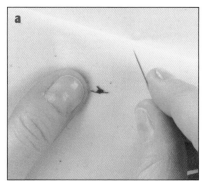

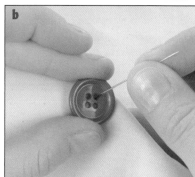

5 Place the needle downward into the hole next to the first. Bring the thread through *without* tightening the thread to the button. Place the toothpick or thick sewing needles under the loop of thread.

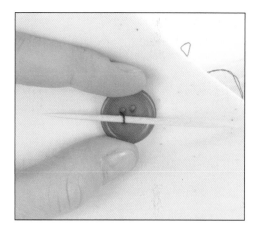

6 If you're sewing a four-hole button, bring the needle up in the empty hole next to where your needle went down in the fabric and down through the last empty hole.

CONTINUED ON NEXT PAGE

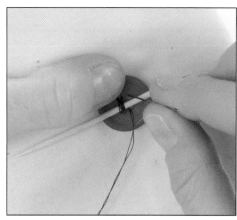

7 Repeat six times on a two- or a four-hole button. On the last stitch, bring the needle through the button to between the button and fabric.

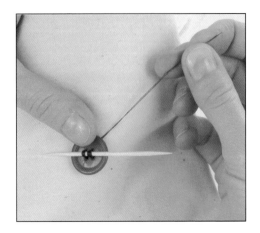

8 Remove the toothpick or thick needle without pulling the needle thread to tighten the thread. Tug the button so that the threads lie against the top of the button and the "spacing thread" is between the button and fabric.

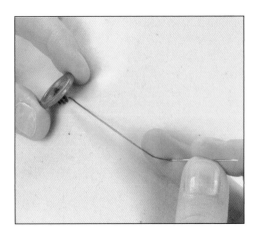

9 Wind the thread firmly around the shank of thread that is under the button. This will create a thread shank between the button and the fabric to allow room for the buttonhole to fit under the button without puckering.

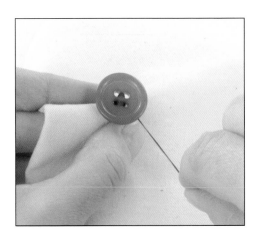

⑩ Backstitch into the shank of thread to secure the thread.

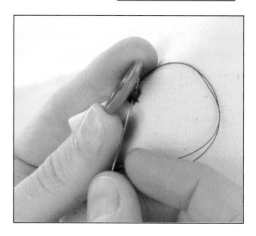

TIP

The thickness of the buttonhole layer of fabric is the key to how fat a toothpick or needle you'll use across the top of the button. A thick wool blazer will require more clearance for the button than a thin blouse will require.

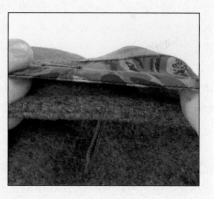

Shank Buttons

Shank buttons are buttons that have a wire loop or plastic shank on the bottom side. They're very well suited for thick fabrics and your best choice for a metal finish button.

Never choose a shank button with a high shank to be sewn on a thin fabric, because the button will flop downward rather than lie flat.

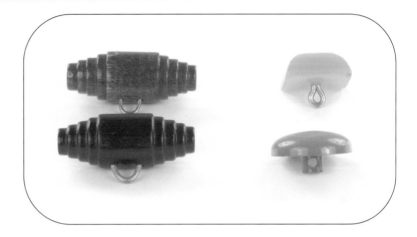

Sew on a Shank Button

① Mark the button placement and anchor the thread as described on pages 147 and 148. Place the button so that the shank of the button will be running the same direction as the buttonhole.

② *For fabric that is not very thick:* Sew the button shank on with small tight stitches to help the button stay upright on the fabric.

③ Anchor the thread between the facing and fabric if possible. If there is no facing, anchor the thread on the back side of the fabric.

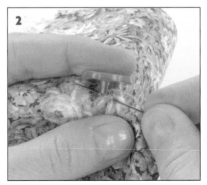

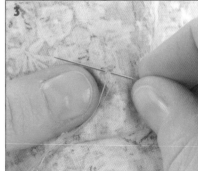

④ *For fabric that is thick:* Sew the shank button on by sewing through the fabric and around the shank of the button while holding the button up from the fabric, or placing a toothpick under the shank of the button. Sew six to eight threads over the shank of the button.

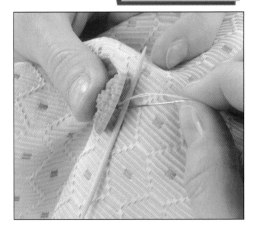

⑤ Bring the needle up from the fabric without going through the shank and wrap the thread securely around the thread to hold the button securely. Knot thread end to secure before clipping thread tail.

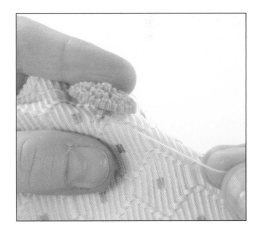

TIP

On loosely woven or delicate fabric, sew a small button to the back side of the fabric behind the button as you sew on the button, to prevent the threads from cutting through the fabric.

Snaps

Snaps are an inconspicuous way to close an opening without making buttonholes. They're available in a variety of sizes and weights. The weight of the snap you choose will correspond with the weight of the fabric you're using.

Sew on a Snap

1. Thread a hand-sewing needle with a double thread. Hide the knot between layers of fabric or on the wrong side of the fabric under the location of the snap. Set the ball portion of the snap in place. Bring the thread to the outer edge of the snap near one of the holes.

2. Push the needle down through the sewing hole on the snap only penetrating the inner layer of fabric so that your stitching will not show on the outside of the garment.

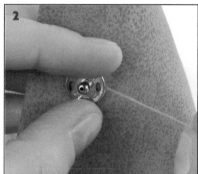

3. Bring the needle up at the edge where you placed the thread at the edge of the snap.

4. Continue making stitches, bringing the needle up through the fabric right next to the previous stitch, gradually moving to the edge of the sewing hole in the snap.

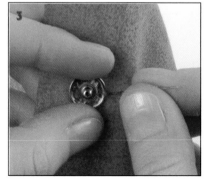

5 Go down through the fabric, and bring the needle up on the outside of the next sewing hole on the snap.

6 Repeat all the way around the snap. Bring the needle back to where you anchored the thread to start between the layers of fabric and knot the thread.

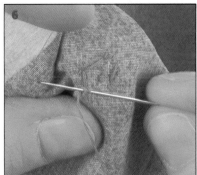

7 Coat the ball of the snap with tailor's chalk.

8 Bring the fabric that will be holding the other side of the snap over on top of the ball portion of the snap, as you will want the fabric to lie when both sides of the snap are attached. Press down on the fabric over the ball of the snap, so that the chalk transfers to the other layer of fabric.

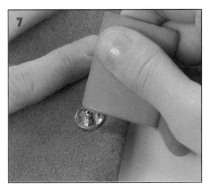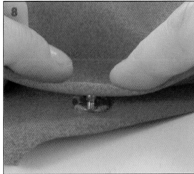

9 Use the transferred chalk mark to place the other side of the snap by placing the chalk mark in the center of the other half of the snap. Sew the second side of the snap the same way you had sewn the ball side of the snap.

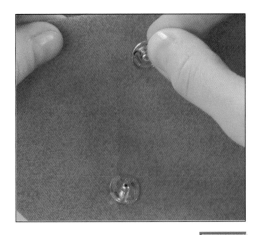

Prong Snaps

Prong snaps are a decorative and strong fastener. A delicate fabric is not a good choice for prong snaps, as the prongs can cut and weaken the fabric.

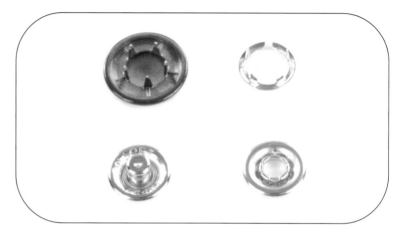

Use Prong Snaps

All prong snaps require some kind of tool to set the snap. Prong snaps have different-size prongs.

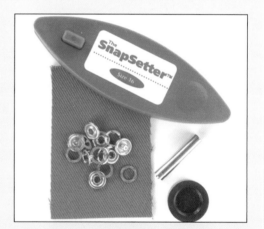

Decorative snaps can make an impact on the appearance of an outfit. They're available in a wide variety of colors and designs.

Always test the reliability of the tool and snaps on a scrap of the fabric, using the same interfacing and thickness of where the snaps will be attached.

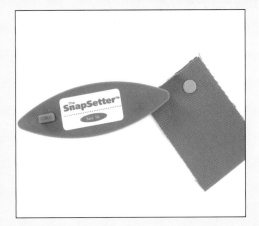

Prong snaps can be used without their counterpart to add a decorative design and make the "real" snap blend into the design.

Be sure to have prong snaps that are long enough to stay held in the fabric. Short prongs might release after being pulled with the other snap and can leave holes that are difficult to mask (a).

Interfacing placed on the back of the fabric helps to stabilize the fabric, adding strength to the fabric where pronged snaps pierce through fibers (b).

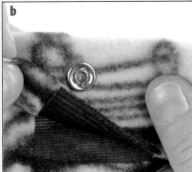

Hook and Eyes

Hook and eyes are a hidden form of a fastener that are generally used on a waistband or neckline.

Hook and eyes come in sets, and the weight and sizes vary. Size 0 is fine and size 3 is heavy. They all perform the same function but in different ways.

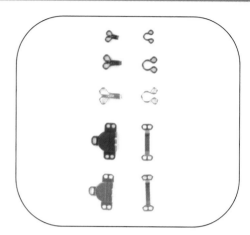

Types of Hook and Eyes

STANDARD HOOK

A standard hook can be used with a straight or a rounded eye. A thread eye can also be used as a hook to connect into.

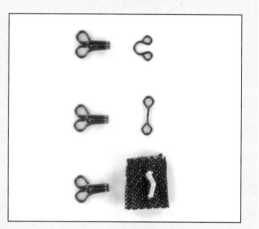

ROUNDED EYES

Rounded eyes are used to close abutted areas. They reduce strain at the top of a zipper even if the zipper comes all the way to the edge.

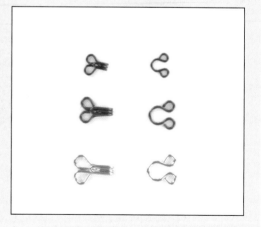

STRAIGHT EYES

Straight eyes are used to join lapped edges. They are hidden and do not distract from a solid fabric look of the garment.

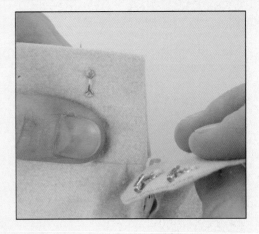

STRONG, FLAT HOOK AND EYES

Strong, flat hook and eyes are designed for the hook to easily slide on and off the eye. They're ideal for overlapping waistbands.

TIP

The size of the hook and eye you choose will depend on the weight of the fabric and the amount of pull on the hook and eye. A tight waistband will need a heavier hook and eye than a secondary fastener at the top of a neckline zipper. Light, standard hooks used to hold a tight waistband will eventually lose their original shape and end up poking the person wearing the garment.

How to Sew Hook and Eyes

You'll rely on the hook and eye to hold a garment closed and lie flat as you intended. Properly sewing them makes this possible.

1 The hook of a hook and eye is always sewn on the inside of the outer layer of an overlapping garment.

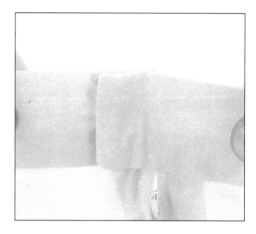

2 Anchor the thread and sew the hook on in the same manner you sew a snap at both loops (see page 152). Anchor the hook under the hook area.

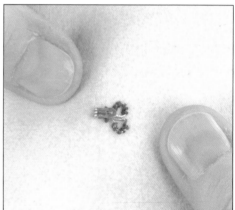

3 Lay the garment closed. With a straight pin, mark the location for the eye on the other layer of fabric.

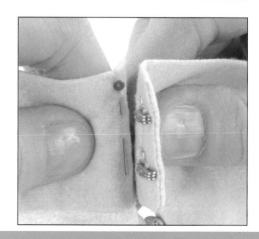

④ Position the eye so it lies over the straight pin.

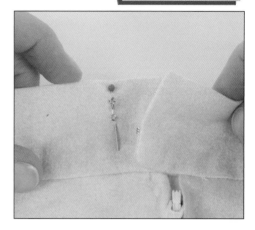

⑤ On lapped edged garments, sew the hook on the inside of the garment. Sew the eye on the right side of the lapped fabric as it is positioned over the pin.

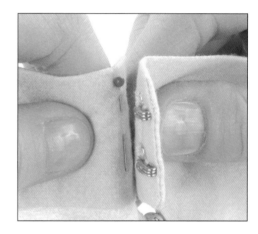

⑥ Place the eye on the hook and overlap the garment edges.

CONTINUED ON NEXT PAGE

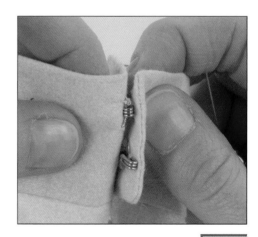

7 A flat hook and eye is a great choice for a waistband.

8 You can also create a thread eye to eliminate the metal eye. Mark where the hook will intersect the eye, and note the width of the hook.

9 Anchor the thread at the outside edge of one marking. Sew three loops of thread leaving the thread loose from the fabric.

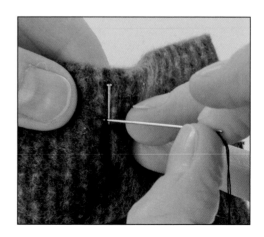

10 Sew blanket stitches over the thread loops (see page 62).

11 Anchor the thread at the opposite end and cut the thread.

TIP

Heavy, flat hook and eye sets are positioned in the same manner as standard hook and eyes. They're sewn on at the openings in the side of each part, but they aren't anchored at the hook.

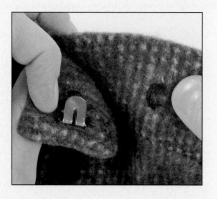

Hook and Loop Tape

Hook and loop tape can be found in a variety of sizes and colors. An assortment of precut hook and loop fasteners are also available.

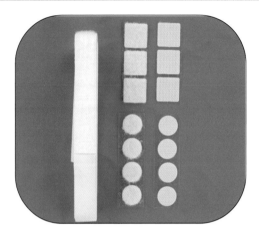

Sew on Hook and Loop Tape

1 Place the hook and loop tape in the desired location. Stitch around the border edges of the tape.

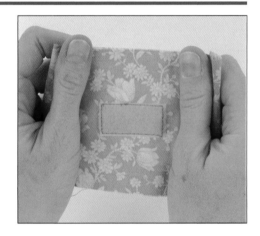

2 To prevent stitching from showing on the opposite side of the fabric, attach the hook and loop tape to a single layer of fabric before joining the fabric together.

3 Machine sewing around the edges of round hook and loop tape can be challenging due to the small circumference. Machine sew an X in the center of the tape, and end with a couple of backstitches for a durable attachment.

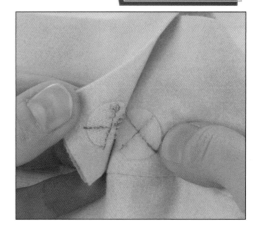

TIP

Hook and loop tape is also available with an adhesive backing, which is ideal for home decorating projects. However, be aware that the adhesive can bleed through some fabrics and gum up your sewing machine needle. Using sew-on hook and loop tape on the fabric side of your project is best.

When making costumes, hook and loop tape is a great shortcut for closing an opening.

chapter **12**

Hemming Techniques

Hemlines change with the seasons. Your wardrobe can last longer with simple hemline changes. In some cases, hems can even be lengthened where you thought there wasn't enough fabric.

SINGER

The amount of hem that is turned will affect the way a curtain or garment hangs. The amount of turned hem is also reliant on the type of fabric used.

The depth of the turned area of the hem will depend on the garment and the fabric (a). The goal is to have the item hang properly.

A straight, flared, pleated, or gathered garment will hold a 1½ to 3-inch hem. Lightweight fabric will require the 3-inch hem to have enough weight in the hem for the fabric to hang properly. Heavier fabric only requires a 2-inch hem (b).

A circular hem requires a 1-inch hem for most fabrics (a). The line of the hem area would be too bulky to have the standard hem. Even the 1-inch hem requires the hem to be eased in to lay smoothly (b).

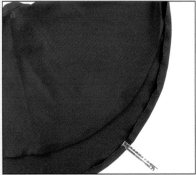

This photo shows examples of an edge stitched hem and a serge rolled hem.

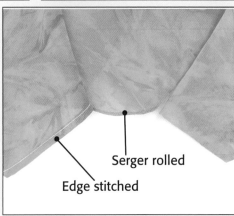

Serger rolled

Edge stitched

Very heavy fabric cannot be turned under without having a very visible press line and uneven bulk (a).

Seam tape is a solution to hemming heavy fabric (b).

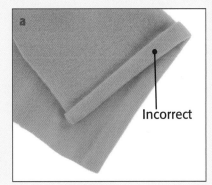

Incorrect

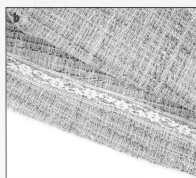

A very full or a curved hem may use a faced hem using bias-cut fabric or bias tape (a).

When you're shortening a ready-made garment, measure the depth of the existing hem before you make any changes (b).

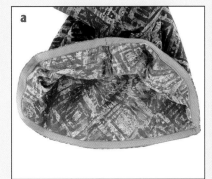

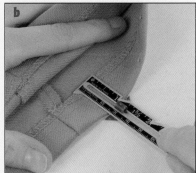

To alter the hem on a pair of jeans, replicate the size of the existing hem as closely as possible. Most jeans have the hem length turned twice to have a stable hem edge.

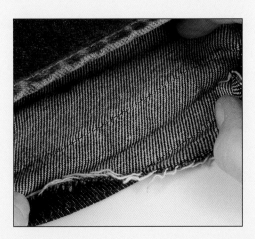

Mark a Garment Hem

The distance from the floor to the desired hem length is a necessary marking. In most cases, it must be marked all the way round the garment with the garment on to achieve a straight hemline. You can spot check the accuracy of your seam with a gauge.

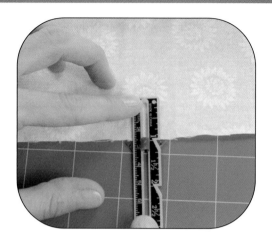

Mark the Hem

1 A straight-edge hem can be marked with the garment on a flat surface after the garment is complete. You may want to try on the garment to make sure the garment hangs evenly all around. Mark one area for length before laying the garment flat to mark the remaining hem.

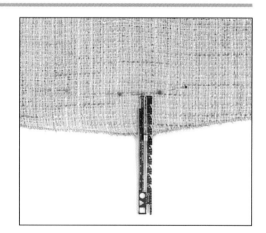

2 Try on the garment with the undergarments and type of shoe you'll be wearing with the garment. Have a friend mark the desired length with chalk markings or straight pins, using a yardstick kept straight and flat to the floor. The photo shows a 1-inch hem.

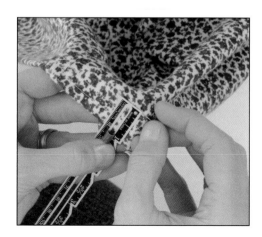

3 If no one is available to mark your hem, try the tools that are available. A hem marking devise or a dress form are great tools when you have no one available. Pants hems are marked using the same method.

> ### TIP
>
> A bias skirt *must* hang for at least 24 hours before you attempt to hem it. This enables the fibers of the fabric to fall into their final hanging position.
>
> If you're altering a hem, remove the original hem and press out all hem lines before beginning a new hem.

Turning the hem after it's marked and preparing the hem edge before sewing in place are necessary elements to a nicely finished edge without any lumps.

1 Turn the hem up at the markings all the way around the garment.

2 Try on the garment to make sure you're happy with the length. Press the turned line of the hem in place. Remove the marking pins as you press.

3 With the skirt hem on a flat surface, use a gauge to mark the hem at the desired hem depth all the way around.

4 Carefully trim away any excess hem fabric.

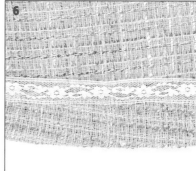

5 Basting the hem in place near the folded edge of the hem will help to maintain the desired hemline.

6 On heavy fabric, apply seam binding to the edge of the hem.

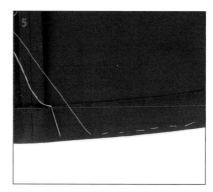

7 Apply a seam finish to the inside edge of the hem. The seam finish that you used in the garment can usually be applied to the hem edge. (See page 95 for seam finish information.)

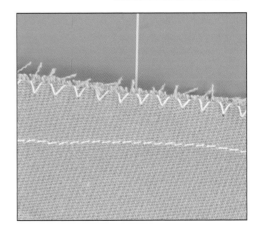

8 It will be necessary to ease in the excess fullness in most hems. To ease in the fullness, sew a line of basting ¼ inch from your seam-finished edge.

9 On a very full skirt, such as a circular hem, you may want to run two rows of basting to help ease in the fullness.

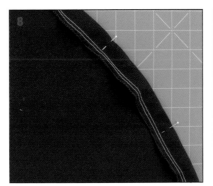 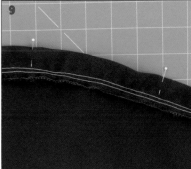

TIP

Although it may seem easier to just make tucks in the hem edge to make it fit the garment, those tucks will eventually show on the outside of the garment as bulk. Leave a narrower hem allowance rather than make tucks.

Sewing a topstitched hem can seem impossible because you can't see the edge of the hem under the fabric. Accurate marking and turning can make the job very easy!

1 Perform all easing and basting described in the previous section. Measure the width of the hem.

2 Use this measurement to set a seam guide on your sewing machine so the stitching will be an ⅛ inch from the inside edge of the hem.

3 Place the hem right side up under the needle and align the folded edge of the hem with your seam guide. Put the sewing machine needle down, and check to be sure the needle is penetrating the hem. Place the presser foot down, and keep the folded edge aligned with the seam gauge. Sew until you meet your beginning stitches.

④ Sew over three to four of the first stitches to secure end of stitching.

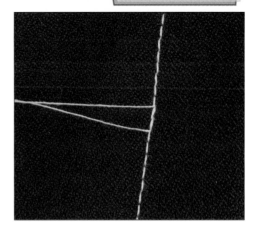

⑤ Repeat a second row of topstitching, if desired, just to the hem side of your first row of stitching. Use the presser foot as a guide to keep the rows of stitching an even distance.

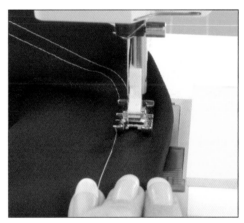

TIP

If your sewing machine has a lock-stitch capability, use a lockstitch at the beginning and end of the topstitching instead of overlapping stitches.

Invisible Hem

Most garments require a hem that is invisible. The stitches aren't noticeable from the outside of the garment. You can create an invisible hem by hand-sewing or with some sewing machines.

1 Perform all easing and basting described in the previous section. Anchor a hand-sewing thread in the inside of the hem at a seam allowance whenever possible to aid in ending the hand sewing.

2 Using a catch-stitch, slipstitch, or blind stitch, pick up one or two threads of the body of the garment directly behind the top of the inside hem edge (see Chapter 5).

3 Continue hand sewing until you reach the end, and anchor the thread in the hem or a seam allowance.

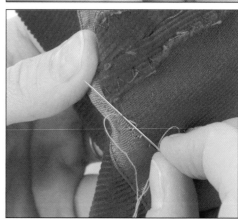

4. Some sewing machines have a built-in blind stitch. It is represented by straight and a zigzag stitch.

5. Prepare the hem as described in the previous section. The photo on the right shows the preferred and easier way to machine blind hem. However a hem with seam tape could be used but takes more experience to handle.

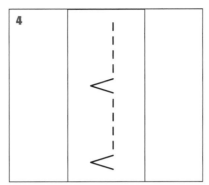 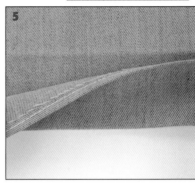

6. Fold the garment back to reveal the hem edge. Allow the straight stitching to fall on the hem allowance and the zigzag stitch to barely catch the garment fabric.

TIP

Always test the machine stitching on scraps of fabric. Prepare the test fabric the same way as the hem you're going to sew. Refer to your sewing machine manual to see what adjustments and guides are available for your machine.

Some garments have curved hemlines, and a faced hem is the neatest way to have a clean edge that will lie smoothly. Patterns with this feature usually include pattern pieces for the curved area to have a facing.

The most common place where a hem facing would be added is to lengthen a garment that does not have fabric available to let the hem down. Typically, you would not have a pattern to follow.

1 Mark the hem as described on page 170. Single-fold bias tape is available in various widths to accommodate the hem depth you want in the garment.

2 Unfold the bias tape and place the fold on the hemline where you want the hem to turn up. Trim the fabric to make the fabric even with the edge of the unfolded bias tape.

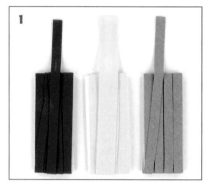

3 Pin the bias tape to the hem edge with right sides together. Use extra tape at the seam to join the ends of the bias tape.

4 Join the ends of the bias tape so that the bias tape fits around the hem edge. Mark the seam.

5 Sew the seam in the bias tape at the marks. Press the seam open.

6 Pin the new seam to the hem edge. Sew the bias tape in the opened fold at the edge of the hem to the body of the garment.

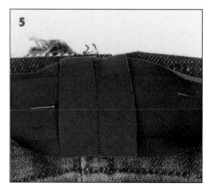

⑦ Grade the seam (see Chapter 9) and under-stitch the facing so that it will stay to the inside of the garment.

⑧ Press the hem to the inside of the garment, and sew the top of the hem tape with hand or machine stitching.

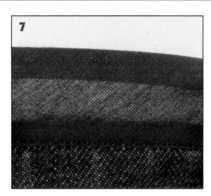

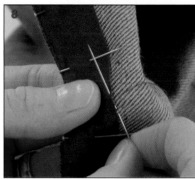

TIP

To eliminate the need for easing, take advantage of seams when adding a bias tape facing. Taper the bias tape seams to fit the garment.

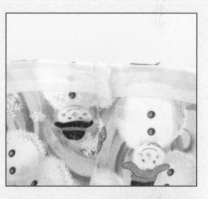

Use different widths of bias tape to achieve the correct hem depth.

Stretchy Knit Hems

Stretchy knit hems, as shown in the photo, require special stitching to prevent stitches from breaking when the fabric is stretched.

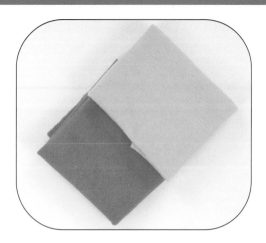

To Sew a Hem on Stretchy Knit

A rolled hem on knit prevents heavy sagging (see photo). A lettuce edge uses the fabric's stretch or crosswise grain to create a decorative edge. The stitching is created by using a medium-width zigzag and stretching the fabric as it's stitched. Be sure to keep an even stretch on the fabric as you sew.

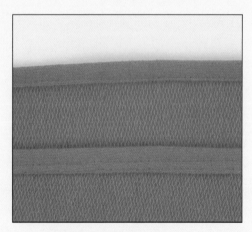

Sewing machines with stitch options may have a stitch represented as three rows of straight stitching (a). This stitch creates a very stretchable straight stitch in a topstitched hem (b).

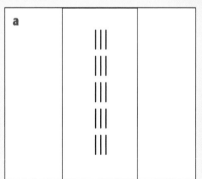

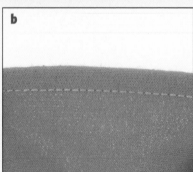

Decorative additions to a hemline allow the hem area to add dimension and detail to a garment.

Add Piping, Lace, and Other Decorative Trim

Piping added to the hem edge of a faced hem, add shaping and the possibility of a colorful addition. Lace and eyelet are delicate additions to loungewear and children's clothing. Adding the lace to the hem allowance before sewing the hem enables the stitching to hold the lace in place, rather than have a row of visible topstitching to hold the lace in place.

Rickrack and decorative trims can be used to hide a worn hemline when a garment hem is let down.

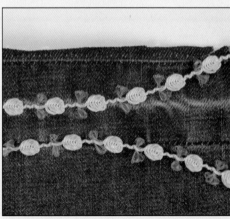

chapter 13

Warm-Up Sewing Projects

Sewing a simple project is the best way to get the feel for how the machine, fabric, thread, and trim work together. Start small before taking on more complex projects. Many beginning projects make great gifts, so you'll be learning to sew while creating gifts that will be cherished by others for years to come.

As you prepare to start any project, always preshrink and press your fabric before cutting out project pieces. Having an item shrink after completion could ruin your finished item by puckering seams and changing the size.

SINGER

Sew a Sachet

Sachets add fragrance and beauty. Nestled between the pillows on a guestroom bed, the sachet keeps the bed fresh and inviting. A sachet also makes a great addition to a bridal-shower gift when filled with bath salts.

Make the Sachet

MATERIALS

9 × 6-inch piece of fabric

9 inches of ½- to 1-inch wide lace or trim to complement fabric

Thread to match the fabric

10 inches of narrow ribbon or lace

Potpourri, lavender, or fragrant filler

Small flowers or decorations to add to the ribbon bow (optional)

ASSEMBLY

1. Stitch on the edge of the single layer of fabric ¼ inch from the raw 9-inch edge. Press the raw edge to the wrong side along the stitch line.

2. Turn the pressed edge under again to enclose the raw edge and press.

3 With the fabric right side up with pressed edge down, align the bottom edge of the lace with the folded, pressed edge. Stitch the lace to the folded edge.

4 Fold the fabric in half, right sides together, matching the 6-inch edges and the folded bottom 9-inch edge that doesn't have the lace edge.

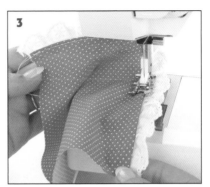
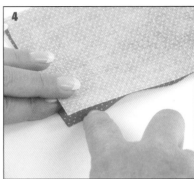

5 Using a ¼-inch seam allowance, sew along the folded 4½-inch bottom edge.

6 Sew the 6-inch edge using a ¼-inch seam allowance, including the lace edge, the same way you stitched the bottom edge. If the fabric is loosely woven and fraying, zigzag the seamed edges as a seam finish. Press the seams as they were sewn.

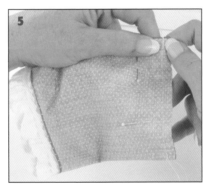
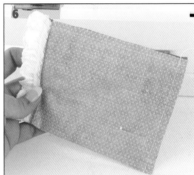

7 Turn the right side out and press the sachet. Press the seams out as far as possible.

8 Fill the sachet two thirds of the way with your chosen filling. Tie closed with ribbon or lace. Embellish the tied ribbon if desired.

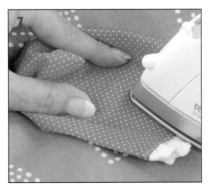
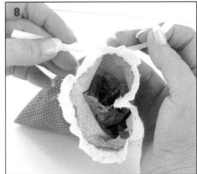

Bottle Gift Bag

Personalize a gift bottle by making a bag with a fabric, which suits the person receiving the gift or with a holiday fabric that reflects the season.

Make the Bottle Gift Bag

MATERIALS

½ yard of fabric, cut one 4-inch circle and one 18 × 20-inch rectangle of fabric

1 yard drawstring

Thread to match the fabric

MARK

① Lay the 18 × 20-inch rectangle on a flat surface, wrong side up.

② On the 20-inch edge, mark 10 inches and 10½ inches from the bottom.

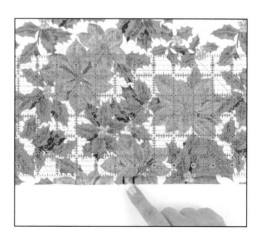

ASSEMBLY

1 Fold the rectangle in half matching the 20-inch edges. Pin into place matching the 10- and 10½-inch markings. Stitch the 20-inch edge using a ¼-inch seam allowance. Leave the area between the markings open for the drawstring to be inserted later.

2 Press the seam allowance open.

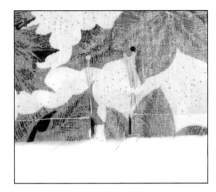

3 Press under ¼-inch on the top edge toward the wrong side of the fabric.

4 Press under another 5 inches. Pin in place, and keep the pins away from the edge and press.

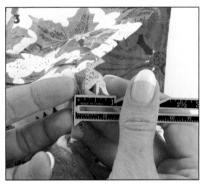

5 Stitch along the pressed-under edge.

6 Stitch ½ to ¾ inch away from the stitching line on the doubled fabric.

CONTINUED ON NEXT PAGE

7 Fold the bag in half on the seam and mark across from the seam. Fold in half again and mark the folds to mark the body of the bag in quarters. Fold the 4-inch circle in half and half again, marking the quarter marks.

8 Sew two rows of basting stitches along the bottom edge of the body of the bag at ½ inch and ¼ inch from the raw edge.

9 Placing right sides together, set the circle inside the bottom of the bag, and match the quarter marks.

⑩ Pull the basting threads to gather the body of the bag and make it fit the edge of the circle.

Note: Hand basting helps to hold the gathers evenly while sewing around a circle.

⑪ Using a ½-inch seam allowance, sew the circle to the body of the bag.

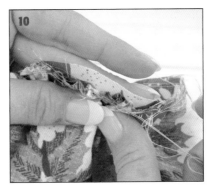
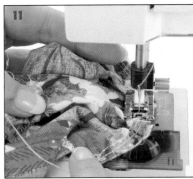

⑫ Turn the right side out and press the bag. Using a safety pin attached to the end of the drawstring, guide the drawstring through the opening left in the seam and into the casing made at the top of the bag.

⑬ Place the bottle in the bag, and pull the drawstring to tighten around the bottle.

Using a tote bag is so much easier than struggling with a bunch of small packages. Consider making your tote bag out of lightweight yet sturdy woven fabric so it can be folded to fit into your purse or suitcase.

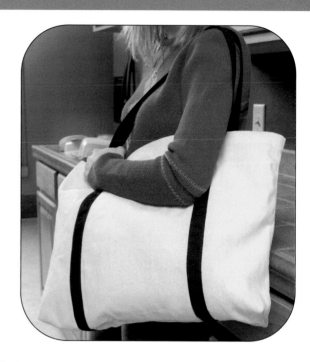

Make the Simple Tote Bag

MATERIALS

½ yard of 45-inch- or 60-inch-wide fabric (almost any woven fabric)

Extra fabric for a pocket (optional)

Thread to match the fabric

3 yards of 1-inch-wide nylon webbing for the straps

CUTTING

1. Trim the selvedge off of the fabric. Cut fabric into two 18 × 22-inch rectangles.

2. To prevent the webbing from unraveling, carefully bring the smoothly cut ends of the nylon webbing to a flame to melt the edges. A slight touch near the flame on the entire end is enough to prevent raveling. Be sure not to melt a lot of the webbing because it will create hard beads of melted nylon.

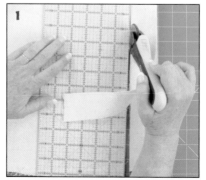

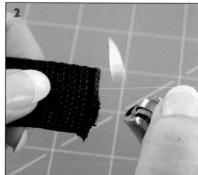

ASSEMBLY

① Place right sides of the fabric together, and sew a seam on one of the 22-inch sides.

② Press the seam as sewn, and zigzag or serge the seam allowance. Press the seam to one side.

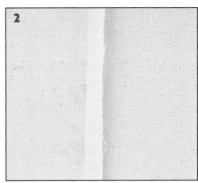

③ Topstitch through the seam allowance on the bag to reinforce the bottom of the bag.

④ Lay the fabric right side up on a flat surface. Fold the webbing in half, and mark the half point.

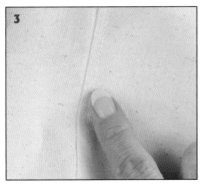

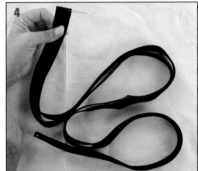

⑤ Place the half mark of the webbing, on the seam of the bag, 5½ inches from one longer edge.

⑥ Pin the webbing in both directions, keeping it 5½ inches from the edges and stopping 4 inches from the end edge.

CONTINUED ON NEXT PAGE

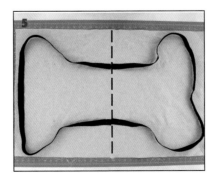

7 Keeping the webbing flat, pin the other side again 5½ inches from the long edge at the seam. Butt the ends of the webbing 5½ inches from the edge. Pin the webbing down flat, keeping it from twisting, and stop 4 inches from each end edge. If you want to add an additional pocket, see page 193 before

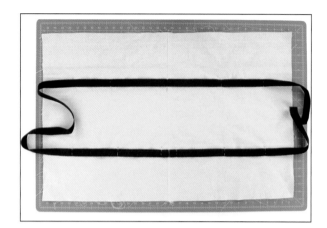

proceeding with step 8 as the pocket goes under the webbing.

8 Zigzag over the butted webbing ends.

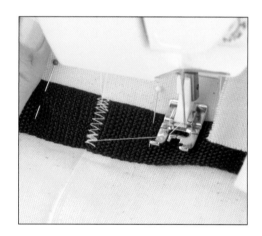

9 Set the machine to straight stitch and sew along the edge of the webbing, starting at the end of the zigzag stitches.

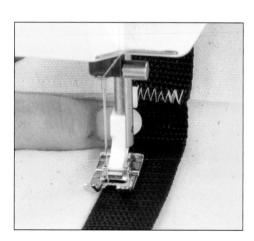

10 Stop at the top 4-inch marking and pivot to sew across the webbing. Because this area gets the most stress, backstitch when you reach the other side of the strap and go forward again to reach the unsewn edge.

11 Repeat for the entire strap, stopping when you reach where you began straight-stitching. Repeat for the other side of the webbing.

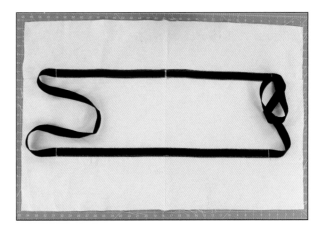

12 Bring the right sides of the fabric together, folding the fabric on the bottom seam line. Pin the sides together. Sew a seam using a ½-inch seam allowance. Repeat for both sides. Zigzag the seam allowance.

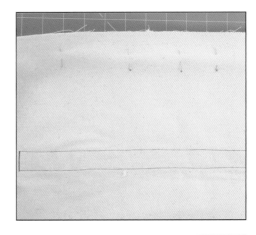

CONTINUED ON NEXT PAGE

13 Press the seams as sewn and then to one side.

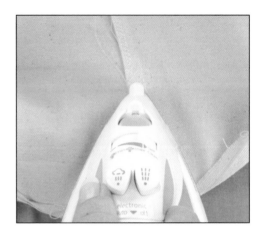

14 Turn under ¼ inch on the top edge of the bag and press. Turn under another 1 inch. Pin and press in place.

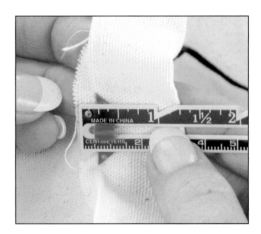

15 Stitch the hem in place. Turn the bag right side out and press from the inside of the bag to prevent melting the straps with the iron.

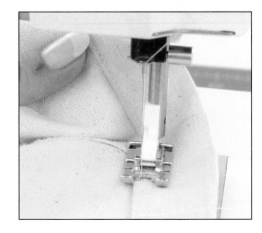

ADD A POCKET

1. Cut a piece of fabric 11 × 12 inches.

2. Place right sides together folding the 12-inch side in half. Sew a seam in the edge that is opposite the folded edge. Turn right side out and press.

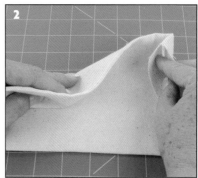

3. Place pocket 7 inches from the top edge of the fabric between the straps and top-stitch across the bottom of the pocket.

4. Pin the pocket flat with the ends of the pocket under the webbing, and continue with sewing down the webbing.

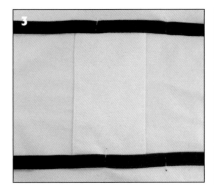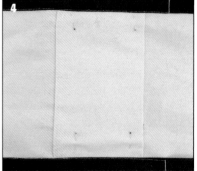

TIP

Square the bottom of the bag by matching the seam with the bottom side seam of the bag. Sew across the triangle evenly on both ends.

Reversible Table Runner

Finding a table runner that suits your tastes can be a challenge. Making your own is very simple!

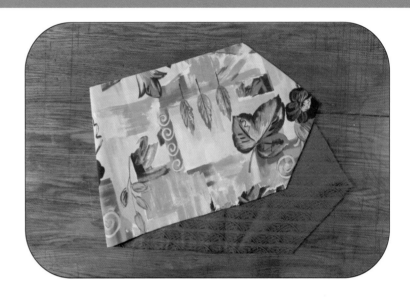

Make the Reversible Table Runner

MATERIALS

36-inch runner: 2 pieces of fabric, ½ yard each, 45 or 60 inches wide

45-inch runner: 2 pieces of fabric, 1½ yards each of 45 inches wide or ½ yard each of 60 inches wide

72-inch runner: 2 pieces of fabric, 2¼ yards each, 45 or 60 inches wide

Thread to match the fabrics

Piping or edge trim (optional)

- 36-inch runner: 2¾ yards
- 45-inch runner: 3¼ yards
- 72-inch runner: 4¾ yards

CUTTING

Note: *Cutting perfect squares is essential when making a table runner. Be sure to start with a straightedge. See Chapter 6 for more information.*

For all runners:

1. Create a straightedge on one cut edge of the fabric.

2. Mark the center of each 17-inch cut edge.

3. Mark 6½ inches up from the 17-inch edge on the longer edge.

4. Using a straightedge, draw a line from the fabric-edge bottom marking to the fabric-edge side markings.

5. Cut off the "triangles."

6. After cutting the rectangles, leave them folded as cut.

For 36-inch runner:

1. Fold the fabric in half, matching the selvedges. Cut a strip 17 inches wide from the straight cut edge. Cut 18½ inches from the fold to create a 17 × 37-inch rectangle when the fabric is unfolded.

For 45-inch runner:

1. Using 45-inch-wide fabric, unfold the fabric from the way it was folded on the bolt. Fold the fabric so the raw edges meet and the selvedges are folded on each side. Cut one rectangle, on the fold that is 17 inches wide on the fold and 23 inches up from the fold. Repeat for the second fabric.

2. Using 60-inch-wide fabric, cut one rectangle 17 inches wide across the fold and 23 inches high from the fold.

For a 72-inch runner:

1. Unfold the fabric from the way it was folded on the bolt. Fold matching the cut ends so that the selvedges are folded.

2. Cut one rectangle of each fabric, 17 inches wide across the fold by 36½ inches up from the fold.

CONTINUED ON NEXT PAGE

ASSEMBLY

All directions include a ½-inch seam allowance.

1 Unfold all cut fabric. Lay each piece on each other to make sure they are cut perfectly identical.

2 Apply optional trim to one fabric, if desired.

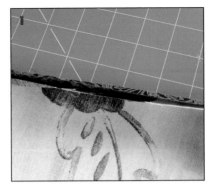

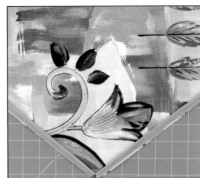

3 Pin fabrics, right sides together, matching all edges.

4 Measure a 6-inch section on the center of one side. Double-pin the ends of the 6-inch area to remind yourself to stop sewing at the double straight pin.

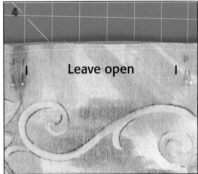

Leave open

5 Starting at a double straight pin, sew the layers together. Backstitch at the start and where you stopped at the second double straight pin.

6 Pivot with the needle down at each corner.

7 Trim the points of the corner seam allowances off.

8 Turn right side out through the 6-inch opening and carefully push out each corner.

 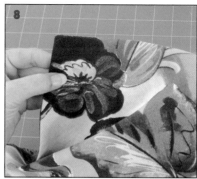

9 Press. Turn under and press seam allowance in the unsewn 6-inch opening.

10 Slipstitch the opening closed. See Chapter 5.

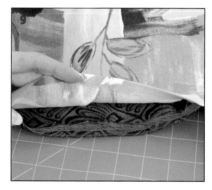 

When you make anything that is reversible, both sides must be identical in order for only one side to show (a). To get double duty out of your table runner, use a holiday fabric on one side and a solid color for everyday use on the other side (b).

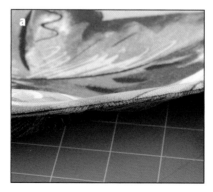 

Reversible Placemats

Finding coordinating table accessories for what you want is easy when you make them yourself.

Make the Reversible Placemats

MATERIALS FOR 4 PLACEMATS

1 yard each of two fabrics

Thread to match the fabrics

12 yards of piping or edge trim (optional)

THE PAPER PATTERN

1. Cut a perfectly square piece of paper in a rectangle 12 × 18 inches.

2. Fold the paper into quarters. Mark 3 inches from the unfolded corner on each edge.

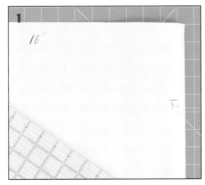

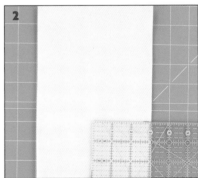

③ Using a round template such as an embroidery hoop or dessert plate, position the template at the edge of the corner to line up with the markings and trace the edge of the template.

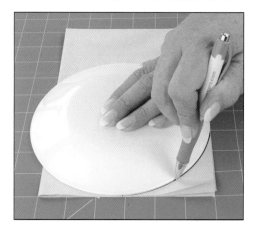

④ Holding all the paper layers perfectly together, trim off the corner using your paper scissors rather than fabric scissors.

⑤ Trace the pattern to make a second pattern piece. Make an identical fold in the second pattern piece.

Note: *Pattern grid material, available in the interfacing section of most fabric stores, will assist in achieving a perfect rectangle.*

CONTINUED ON NEXT PAGE

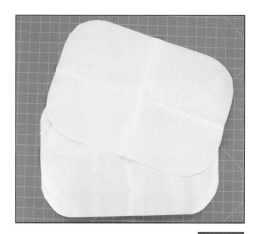

Reversible Placemats *(continued)*

CUTTING

1 Using the fold lines in the paper as grain-line markings, place the pattern on the fabric. Keep the grain line evenly parallel with the selvedge of the fabric.

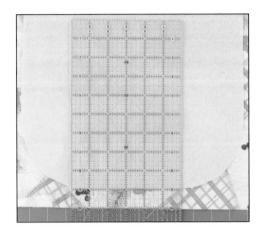

2 Pin the pattern smoothly onto the fabric.

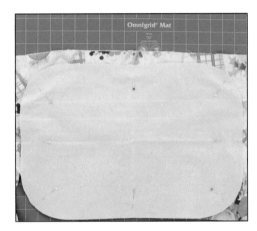

3 Cut the fabric at the edge of the pattern pieces. Repeat for the second fabric.

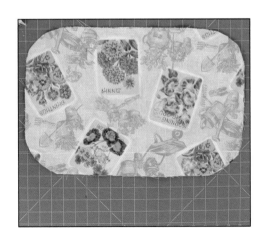

ASSEMBLY

All assembly uses ¼-inch seam allowance.

1 Unpin and lay the pieces on top of each other to check that they are identical (a). Trim can be applied to one layer of the fabric (b), if desired.

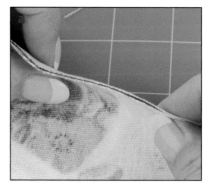

2 Align edges with right sides together and pin in place.

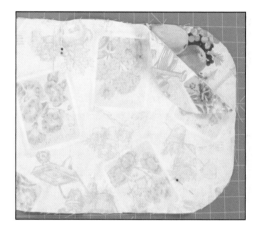

3 Measure a 4-inch section on one edge of each placemat and insert double straight pins at the beginning and end of this section. These pins will serve as a reminder to stop sewing to leave an opening for turning the placemat right sides out.

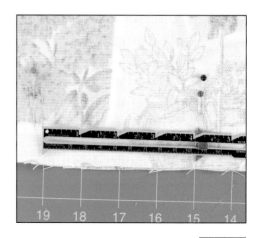

4 Sew the edges leaving the 4-inch area unsewn.

5 Press as sewn.

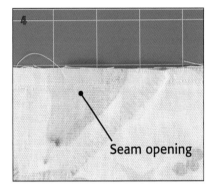

Seam opening

6 Turn right side out by pulling the fabric through the 4-inch opening.

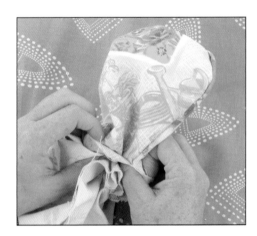

7 Press flat and turn under the 4-inch opening.

8 Slipstitch opening closed. See chapter 5 for instructions.

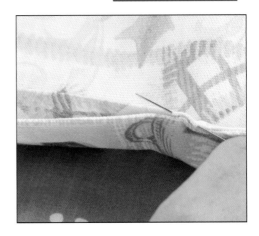

9 Optional: Topstitch ¼-inch from the edge.

10 Repeat to make the other three placemats.

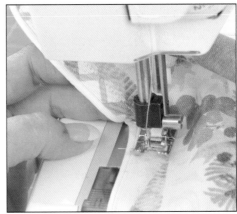

TIP

Experiment with the stitches available on your sewing machine to add a decorative touch to your topstitching.

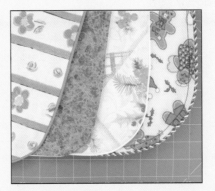

Cloth Napkins

Cloth napkins are simple to make yet cost a small fortune. Make them yourself to match your table setting or occasion.

Make the Cloth Napkins

MATERIALS FOR 4 NAPKINS

1 yard of 45-inch-wide fabric (60-inch-wide fabric will yield 6 napkins)

Thread to match the fabric

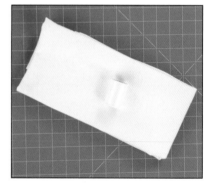

CUTTING

1 Match selvedge edges of the fabric.

2 Cut four 18-inch squares.

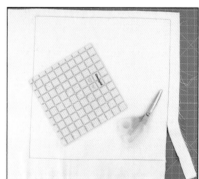

ASSEMBLY FOR SQUARE NAPKIN

1 Turn under and press ¼ inch on all edges.

2 Press under another ¼ inch, enclosing the raw edge of the fabric.

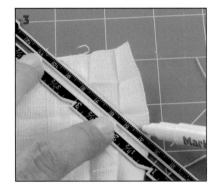

3 To miter the corners, unfold the pressed edges and place a straightedge across the corner from fold line to fold line, as shown in the figure. Draw a line and cut on the line.

4 Turn the corner in, parallel to the cut line, using the pressed lines as a guide.

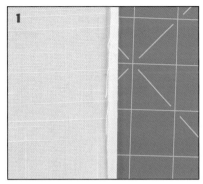
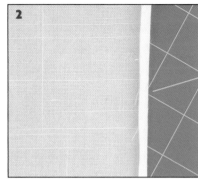

5 Turn the sides again on the fold lines to form a perfect corner. Slipstitch the edges of the corner to hold them snug to each other.

6 Repeat for all corners. Topstitch the hem pivoting at the corners. Repeat the process for other napkins.

CONTINUED ON NEXT PAGE

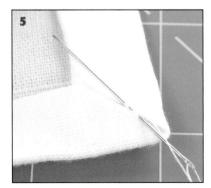

ASSEMBLY FOR ROUNDED-CORNER NAPKIN

1 Cut each napkin, as previously described on page 204. Use a round template to round off the corners.

2 *Option 1:* Satin-stitch the edge of the napkin by setting your sewing machine to a shortened zigzag stitch and stitch around the napkin.

3 *Option 2:* Sew a basting line of stitching ¼ inch from the edges.

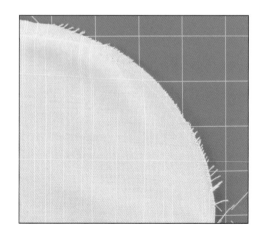

④ Press along the stitching to one side of the napkin. Turn under and press again.

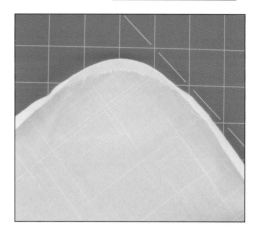

⑤ Use basting stitches to ease in the excess fabric and make the hem lie smoothly.

⑥ Hand-slipstitch or hand-topstitch the hem.

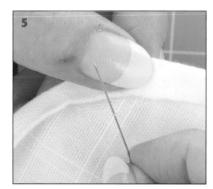

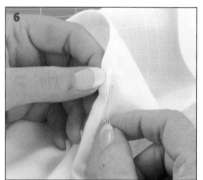

TIP

Sergers offer you the option of sewing a perfect decorative rolled hem on your napkins.

Baby Receiving Blanket

Anyone who has had a baby will tell you that there is no such thing as too many receiving blankets. Making your own allows you to make them a bit larger than most purchased receiving blankets.

Make the Baby Receiving Blanket

MATERIALS
1¼ yards of 45-inch-wide flannel
Thread to match the fabric

ASSEMBLY

1 Fold the fabric in quarters and trim to remove the selvedge to make it square.

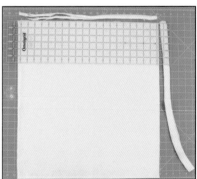

② Turn under edges ¼ inch and ¼ inch again.

③ Create mitered corners (see page 205).

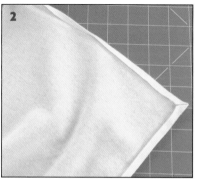

④ Sew down the hem by machine or slipstitch for a softer edge.

TIP

Experiment with threads and your machine's stitches to create a beautiful hem on a plain blanket.

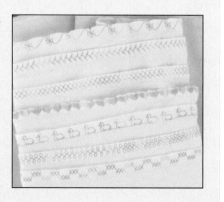

Balloon Window Valance

In addition to saving you money, sewing allows you to have more choices for your window dressings than those available in retail stores and catalogs. The following instructions are for a 14 × 43-inch valance, which will be approximately 12 inches long once it is "puffed." Most windows will require at least two of this measurement to achieve fullness across the window.

Make the Balloon Window Valance

MATERIALS

1 yard of 45-inch wide fabric

Optional: Buy 2 yards and cut into two panels. Seam them on one end to make a 36 × 90-inch panel and sew as one panel to create a wider valance.

Thread to match the fabric

CUTTING

1. Fold the fabric as it was on the bolt with the selvedges meeting. Trim the cut edge of the fabric to square it with the fold. Squarely remove the selvedge. (See Chapter 6 for more information on squaring fabric).

2. Measure 29 inches up from the original cut edge of the fabric (the long edge). Cut on the 29-inch marking so that you have 29 inches by the width of the fabric rectangle.

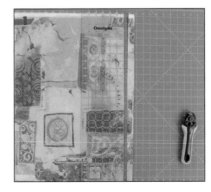

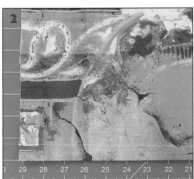

ASSEMBLY

1 Match the long edges with the right sides of the fabric together. Sew a ½-inch seam. Apply seam finish to prevent fraying in the laundry. Press seam open.

2 Hem the 29-inch edges by turning them under ¼ inch and ¼ inch again to enclose the raw edges. Stitch in place.

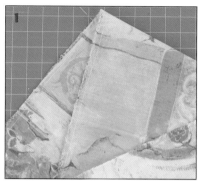
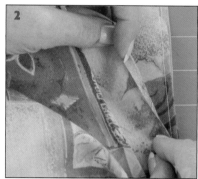

3 Turn right side out and place seam 6 inches from the top folded edge.

4 Press to crease at the top fold.

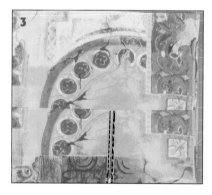

5 Topstitch 3 inches and 4½ inches from the top pressed edge for the rod pocket.

Note: Press the bottom of the balloon without making a crease to make fluffing the tube easier.

Straight Window Curtain

Accurate measuring and straight sewing makes curtains an easy home decorating project.

Determine the Panel Requirements

LENGTH OF THE CURTAIN

- A Height of window: Curtain rod to the desired length
- B Plus 2 inches for header
- C Plus 4½ inches for the back of the header and rod pocket
- D Plus 3½ inches for hem
- E Total length of curtain fabric needed per panel

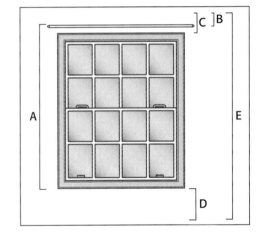

WIDTH OF THE CURTAIN

- Measure distance across the window or curtain rod. One and a half times the width of the window will give you enough fullness for a straight curtain.
- You will want a fuller curtain if you plan on tying it back. Double the width of the window will usually give you enough for a tied-back curtain.
- Allow 1 inch on each side of each panel for side hems.
- Seam lengths of fabric if necessary to create fabric to the desired width of the curtain panel.

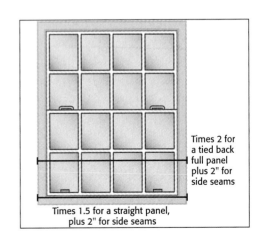

Times 2 for a tied back full panel plus 2" for side seams

Times 1.5 for a straight panel, plus 2" for side seams

PURCHASING YOUR FABRIC

Divide the length of your panels by 36 inches to determine how many yards of fabric you will need. Then multiply the number of yards by the number of panels you'll need. Allow extra fabric when a fabric has a repeating design, such as plaids, floral designs, or horizontal stripes is being used to make more than one panel. The repeating design will need to line up evenly on all of the curtain panels. Also, remember to add in fabric if you are using more than one width of fabric per panel.

Because a curtain panel can seem like a big square of fabric, take a moment before you start moving the fabric to pin a piece of paper with the word *top* on it to the top of each curtain panel. This is especially helpful when using a one way design fabric.

Standard Curtain Measurements		
Finished Curtain Length	*Yardage for Each Panel**	*Cut One for Each Panel*
15-inch valance	¾ yard	25 inches × width
24-inch panel	1 yard	34 inches × width
30-inch panel	1¼ yards	40 inches × width
36-inch panel	1⅓ yards	46 inches × width
45-inch panel	1¾ yards	55 inches × width
54-inch panel	2 yards	64 inches × width
63-inch panel	2¼ yards	73 inches × width
72-inch panel	2½ yards	82 inches × width
84-inch panel	2¾ yards	94 inches × width
90-inch panel	3 yards	100 inches × width

*when using 45-inch-wide faric and non-repeating prints

CUTTING

Always keep your measurements square to prevent lopsided curtains and uneven hems. See page 75 on rotary cutting and rulers.

CONTINUED ON NEXT PAGE

Make the Straight Window Curtain

ASSEMBLY

1 Press under ½ inch on the top and bottom of the panel.

2 Press under ¼ inch on the sides of each panel.

3 Press under each side another ¾ inch, enclosing the ½ inch that was pressed under on the top and bottom.

4 Topstitch, blind stitch, or slipstitch the side hems in place.

5 On the top of the panel, press under 4 inches.

6 Stitch the turned-under edge.

7 Topstitch 2 inches from the top pressed edge.

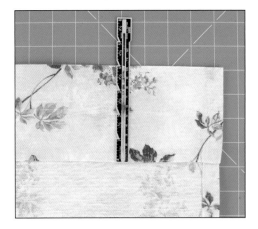

8 Turn and press under 3 inches on the bottom of the curtain panel.

9 Slipstitch, blind stitch, or topstitch the hem in place. The long straight hem in curtains is a great place to experiment with using your sewing machine blind stitch. Insert curtain rod in casing stitched in the top hem in step 7.

More Sewing Projects

Now that you've accomplished mastering the basics, try your hand at larger projects. Taking things one step at a time makes them easy!

SINGER

Pillow with a Zipper

Making pillow covers with a zipper allows you to remove them for laundering as well as to reuse the pillow forms. Use the forms to update your décor or simply change with the season. Change the color of your accent pillows to transform the room. The following directions will make your pillow cover an inch smaller than the form, which creates a completely filled, plump pillow.

Make the Pillow with a Zipper

MATERIALS

Thread to match the fabric

Pillow Form	45 Inches Wide Fabric	Zipper
12 inches	½ yard	10 inches
14 inches	½ yard	12 inches
16 inches	½ yard	14 inches
18 inches	½ yard	16 inches
20 inches	⅝ yard	18 inches
24 inches	1 yard	22 inches

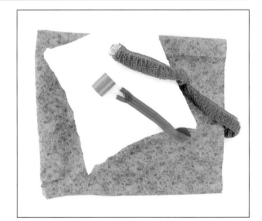

Piping or set in edge trim (optional)

Pillow Form	Piping or Edge Trim
12-inch pillow	1⅓ yards
14-inch pillow	1⅔ yards
16-inch pillow	1⅞ yards
18-inch pillow	2 yards
20-inch pillow	2¼ yards
24-inch pillow	2⅔ yards

CUTTING

Pillow Form	Front	Back *Cut One of Each Measurement*
12-inch pillow	12-inch square	10 × 12 inches 6 × 12 inches
14-inch pillow	14-inch square	11 × 14 inches 7 × 14 inches
16-inch pillow	16-inch square	12 × 16 inches 8 × 16 inches
18-inch pillow	18-inch square	13 × 18 inches 9 × 18 inches
20-inch pillow	20-inch square	14× 20 inches 10 × 20 inches
24-inch pillow	24-inch square	16 × 24 inches 12 × 24 inches

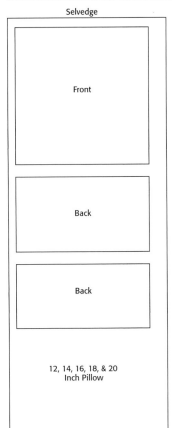

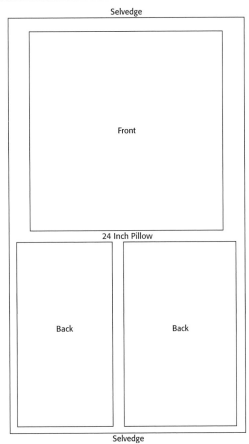

CONTINUED ON NEXT PAGE

ASSEMBLY

Note: Use ½-inch seam unless directions indicate otherwise.

1. Place the zipper face down on the right side and center on a "width of the pillow" edge of the smaller pillow back edge. (On a 12-inch edge for a 12-inch pillow, 14-inch edge for a 14-inch pillow, and so on) Using a zipper foot, sew the zipper to the fabric along the zipper guideline. Apply a seam finish to the raw edge.

2. Press the fabric back with the zipper tape under the body of the fabric. Stitch close to the folded edge.

3. Place the other side of the zipper along the edge of the other "pillow width edge" back piece, right sides together with the raw edge of the fabric and the zipper tape even. Align the side edges of both back pieces. Sew along the zipper tape guideline and apply a seam finish to the raw edge.

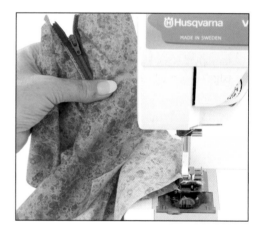

4. Lay the back piece out flat and place the back pieces on top of the front piece with the right sides together. Fold under the larger sewn back so that the back becomes the same size as the front, and a flap is formed over the zipper. Pin the newly formed tuck evenly across the zipper tape (on just the back piece). Keep the back the same size and square to the front piece. Set the front piece aside.

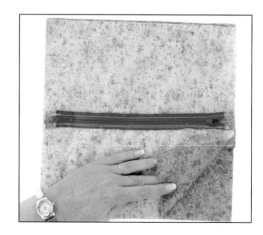

⑤ Using the zipper foot again, stitch on the zipper tape of the larger back piece front on the wrong side. Stitch along the zipper tape guide to hold the tuck in place. Press the back.

⑥ Baste the zipper flap at the side edges so that it covers the zipper and will be held in place during the assembly of the pillow.

⑦ At this stage, you can apply the optional piping or set in edge finish to the front panel.

⑧ Open the zipper and place the front and back right sides together. Align all the edges. Pin or baste in place.

⑨ Sew pivoting at corners using a ½-inch seam allowance. Apply a seam finish.

⑩ Turn right side out through the open zipper, press, and stuff with the pillow form.

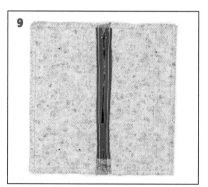
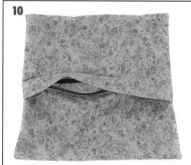

Round Pillow with a Zipper

Round pillows break up monotony and add dimension to a setting. Sewing your own allows you to have the colors you want without breaking the bank.

Materials are all the same as for a square pillow except, you will need a round pillow form.

Make the Round Pillow with a Zipper

1 Follow all directions for a square pillow up to and including step 6. Using a round template the size of your pillow form or a compass, mark a circle on the square.

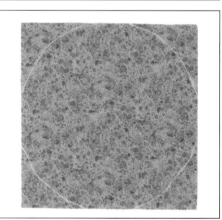

2 Trim on the marked line.

3 Baste the edges of the zipper flap.

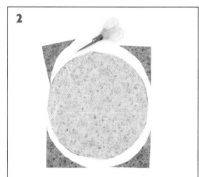

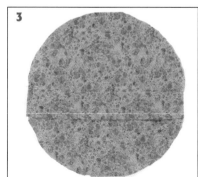

④ Sew the optional piping or trim to the front edge. Open the zipper. Lay the back panel on the front panel, right sides together, matching the edges.

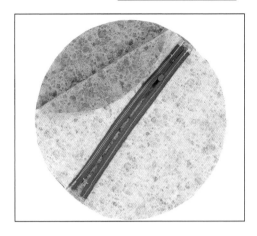

⑤ Pin or baste in place.

⑥ Sew the panels together using a ½-inch seam allowance.

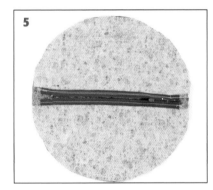
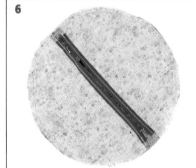

⑦ Turn right sides out through the zipper. Press and stuff with the pillow form.

Messenger Bag

Fabric choices and embellishments are unlimited. In the right fabric, even guys will carry messenger bags to hold their paraphernalia. Use appliqués, snaps, and trims to make your bag anything you want it to be.

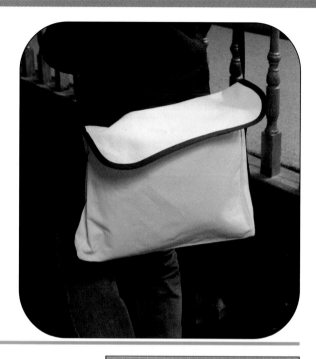

Make the Messenger Bag

MATERIALS

½ yard fabric: cotton duck, canvas, denim, or nylon

Thread to match the fabric

1 package extra-wide double-fold bias tape

2 yards of 1-inch wide nylon webbing

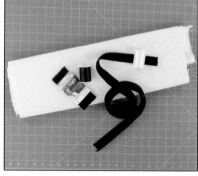

CUTTING

Cut one 34 × 17-inch rectangle, body

Cut two 12 × 4-inch rectangles, sides

Cut two 17 × 4-inch rectangles, bottom

① Fold 34 × 17-inch rectangle in half lengthwise. Mark 3 inches in each direction from the unfolded corner.

② Use a round paper template or dessert plate to round off the corner between the markings.

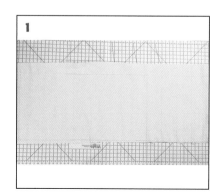

ASSEMBLY

1 Carefully fuse the ends of the webbing with a flame without making any beads of melted nylon or seal with a seam sealant or clear nail polish.

2 Keeping the webbing flat, center it on top of each side of the rectangle, and align the ends of the webbing with the ends of the rectangle. Pin webbing into place.

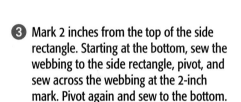

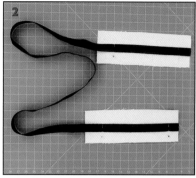

3 Mark 2 inches from the top of the side rectangle. Starting at the bottom, sew the webbing to the side rectangle, pivot, and sew across the webbing at the 2-inch mark. Pivot again and sew to the bottom.

4 Starting at the unrounded end, measure and mark 11½ inches down the side and 3 inches from the 11½-inch mark on each side of the body of the bag.

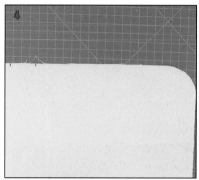

5 Sew a row of basting on the ½-inch seam line just past each marking. Clip the seam allowance on the 11½-inch and 3-inch marks.

6 Starting at the unrounded edge, pin or baste the side of the bag to the body of the bag with right sides together. Pivot the body of the bag at each snipped seam allowance. Sew the side to the body of the bag using a ½ seam allowance. Repeat for the other side of the bag. Add a seam finish to the seam allowances.

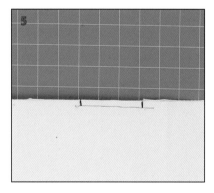

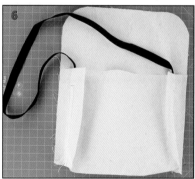

CONTINUED ON NEXT PAGE

7 Starting at the top of the seam allowance, sew ½ inch from the edge of the curved flap of the bag.

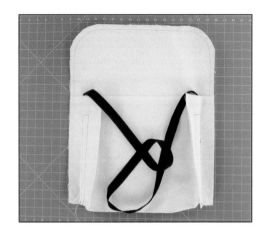

8 Trim the flap at the stitching line to remove ½ inch of fabric.

9 Press the seam allowances in on the side of the bag toward the sides.

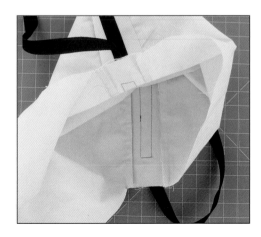

10 Starting at the center of the front of the body of the bag, apply bias tape to the top edge of the bag, keeping the narrower edge of the bias tape to the outside of the bag. Pin or baste in place. Turn under and overlap the bias tape when you reach where it starts. Sew on the bias tape (see pages 124 and 125).

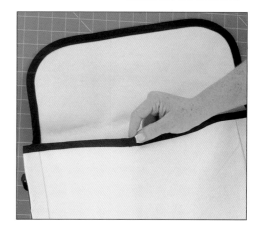

11 Fold the center of each side of the bag inward and crease at the halfway mark. Topstitch across the bias tape, ½ inch from the fold, to help the sides stay folded inward.

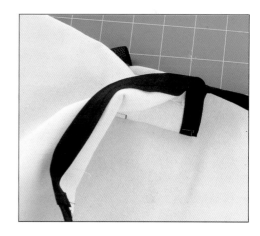

12 **Bag Bottom:** Sew 17 × 14-inch rectangles, right sides together, leaving an opening for turning. Turn right side out. Slipstitch the opening closed. Press and place in the bottom of the bag.

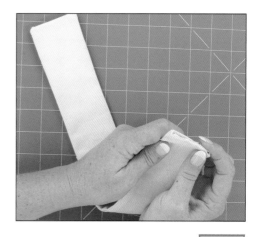

Small Pouch with a Zipper

Toiletries, game pieces, and pencils and pens are just some of the many uses for this pouch. Kids like having their own toiletry bag when staying for overnight visits. Make one for every member of your family so there are no squabbles over who owns what.

Make the Small Pouch with a Zipper

MATERIALS

¼ yard fabric: cotton, nylon, washable fabric

9-inch zipper

Thread to match the fabric

CUTTING

Cut two 10½ × 7-inch rectangles

ASSEMBLY

1 Place the zipper face down and centered on one of the 10½-inch edges. Using a zipper foot, sew the zipper to the fabric by sewing on the guideline on the zipper tape.

2 Fold and press the fabric and zipper tape under the body of the fabric. Topstitch near the fold to hold the back from being caught in the zipper.

3 Repeat for the other side of the zipper on the 10½-inch edge of the other rectangle.

4 Open the zipper. Place the right sides of the rectangle together. Sew all three edges using a ½-inch seam allowance. Apply a seam finish.

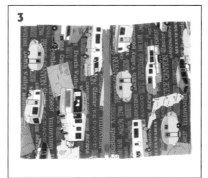

5 With the side seam up, mark 1 inch from the end of the seam and stitch across the marking.

6 Repeat step 4 on the other bottom corner. Turn the bag right side out, close the zipper and press.

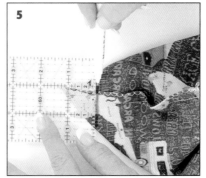

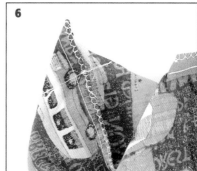

Flanged Pillow Sham

Adding accents of color can enhance any room. Pick a solid or a print to complement your bedding.

Make the Flanged Pillow Sham

MATERIALS   Thread to match the fabric

Pillow Size	Fabric for Each Sham	Cutting
Standard, 20 × 26 inches	1⅝ yards	1 front, 27 × 33 inches 2 backs, 27 × 20 inches
Queen, 20 × 30 inches	1⅝ yards	1 front, 27 × 37 inches 2 backs, 27 × 22 inches
King, 20 × 36 inches	2⅝ yards	1 front, 27 × 43 inches 2 backs, 27 × 25 inches

CUTTING

Lay fabric out in a single thickness. Cut out pieces as shown in the photo.

ASSEMBLY

1 Press under ½ inch and ½ inch again on one 27-inch edge of each back piece. Stitch in place.

2 Lay back piece on front piece, right sides together with the hemmed edge in the center. Line up the corners and edges.

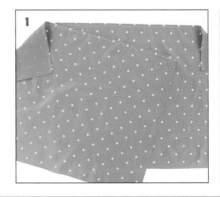

③ Lay the other back piece on the other end, lining up the other corners and edges. Pin in place.

④ Sew the edges using a ½-inch seam allowance and pivoting at the corners. Trim the corners. Press.

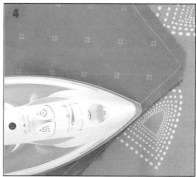

⑤ Turn right side out. Press so all seams are at the edges.

⑥ Pin back sections flat, keeping pins 3 inches from the edge. Mark 3 inches from each corner with a temporary mark.

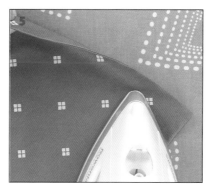

⑦ Set a seam guide on your sewing machine for 3 inches from the needle.

⑧ Topstitch 3 inches from the edges of the pillow sham, pivoting at corner marks. Meet and overlap your first stitching by a few stitches. Press.

Tabbed Valance and Curtain

Curtain rods are available in a variety of forms and shapes. Why hide them under a curtain? You don't if you make tabbed window coverings.

Make a Tabbed Valance and Curtain

MATERIALS

Thread to match the fabric

Fabric amount as shown in chart. Allow extra for more than one panel if your fabric has a repeat design that must horizontally match one of the panels.

Finished Curtain Length	Yardage for Each Panel	Cut One for Each Panel	Cut One for Each Facing	Cut Tabs
15-inch valance	¾ yard	15½ inches × width	3 inches × width	7½ × 4 inches
24-inch panel	1 yard	24½ inches × width	3 inches × width	7½ × 4 inches
30-inch panel	1¼ yards	30½ inches × width	3 inches × width	7½ × 4 inches
36-inch panel	1½ yards	36½ inches × width	3 inches × width	7½ × 4 inches
45-inch panel	1¾ yards	45½ inches × width	3 inches × width	7½ × 4 inches
54-inch panel	2 yards	54½ inches × width	3 inches × width	7½ × 4 inches
63-inch panel	2¼ yards	63½ inches × width	3 inches × width	7½ × 4 inches
72-inch panel	2½ yards	72½ inches × width	3 inches × width	7½ × 4 inches
84-inch panel	2¾ yards	84½ inches × width	3 inches × width	7½ × 4 inches
90-inch panel	3 yards	90½ inches × width	3 inches × width	7½ × 4 inches

Mark and cut out your fabric. For the tabs, cut strips 4 inches by the width of the fabric. Follow the directions to achieve finished tabs. The photos in this section are of a 15-inch valance being constructed.

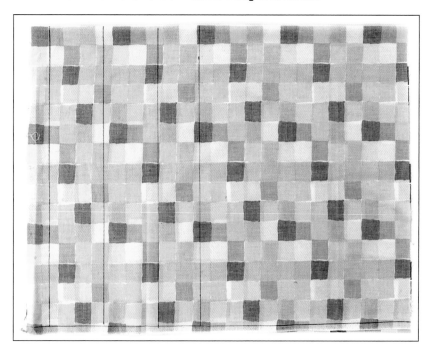

ASSEMBLY

1 Turn and press under ½ inch twice on each side of the main panel. Stitch in place.

2 Matching the hemmed edges, fold the panel in half and repeat folding in half until the fabric is approximately 6 inches wide. Mark each fold for the placement of a tab at the top of the panel.

CONTINUED ON NEXT PAGE

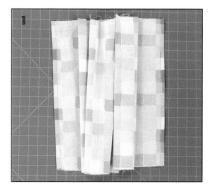

3 Fold the length of the 4-inch strip for the tabs in half. Place right sides together and sew a ½-inch seam on the raw edge (a). Turn right side out. A large safety pin is one of the ways to hold on the end while turning (b).

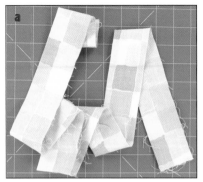

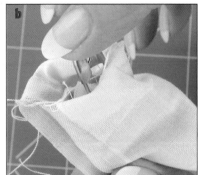

4 Press the tube with the seam stitching perfectly to the side edge.

5 Topstitch ⅛ to ¼ inch from both edges of the tube.

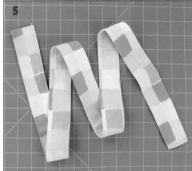

TIP

To make turning fabric right side out a little easier, make a few stitches in the end of a long strip and use a dowel to help turn the fabric.

6 Cut the tube into 7½ inch lengths to form individual tabs.

7 Fold the tabs in half, center the tabs on the marks made at the top of the panel, and pin them into place. Align the end tabs with the end hem.

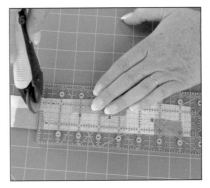
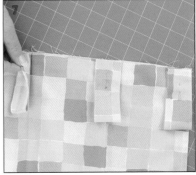

8 Baste the tabs in place.

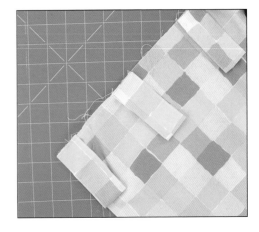

9 Press under ½ inch on one long edge of the 3-inch facing. Use a line of stitching as a guide if desired.

CONTINUED ON NEXT PAGE

10 Starting in the center of the facing and center of the panel so that the facing ends will evenly extend beyond the ends of the panel. Pin the other long edge of the 3-inch facing to the top of the panel, wrong sides together, matching the raw edges. Stitch using a ½-inch seam allowance.

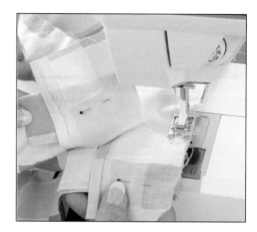

11 Press the seam to the facing side. If you're working with a bulky fabric, see pages 118 and 119 for instructions on how to grade the seam.

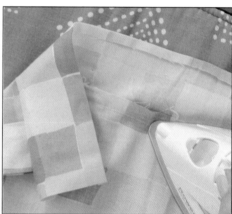

12 Under-stitch (see pages 120 and 121) the joined edge of the facing. Turn under the ends of the facing and press.

13 Pin the facing down to the panel. Stitch in place.

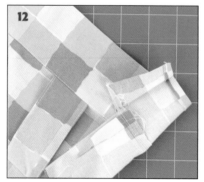

⑭ Turn under ½-inch on hem edge of panel. Use a line of stitching as a guide if preferred to measuring.

⑮ Turn up a 3-inch hem, press, and stitch in place.

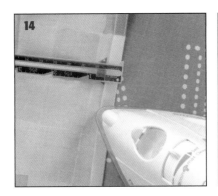

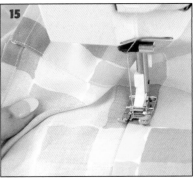

TIP

Change the look of a tabbed valance by not enclosing the end of one tab in the seam and adding buttons or buckles to hold them in place.

Hostess Apron

Trendy aprons are perfect for the hostess of any party and will keep your clothes clean while busy in the kitchen. You can make aprons in holiday fabric as gifts or for a festive touch to serving your holiday meals.

Make the Hostess Apron

MATERIALS

1¼ yards of 45-inch cotton fabric

Thread to match the fabric

CUTTING

Cut 26 × 3½-inch waistband

Cut two 5 × 32-inch ties

Cut 40 × 23-inch body of the apron

ASSEMBLY

1 Clean-finish the 32-inch edges and one 5-inch edge of each tie by turning under ¼ inch and ¼ inch again and stitch in place.

2 Fold waistband in half lengthwise with wrong sides together. Press and mark the center fold. Mark ½ inch from each 3½-inch edge. Set the waistband aside.

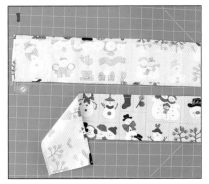
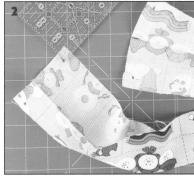

3 Turn under ¼ inch of each 23-inch edge of the 40 × 23-inch body of the apron and press. Turn under another ½ inch and press

4 Stitch the pressed edge.

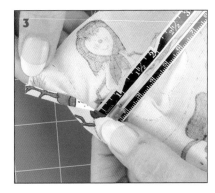

5 Turn under a ¼-inch edge of a 40-inch edge. Turn up 2 inches and press.

6 Stitch in place.

CONTINUED ON NEXT PAGE

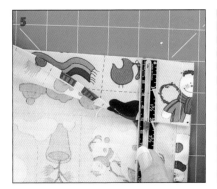

7 Mark the center of the unsewn 40-inch edge. Sew two rows of basting on the other 40-inch edge, less than ½ inch from the raw edge of the fabric.

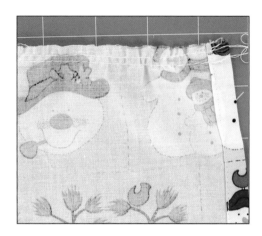

8 Place the basted edge of the body of the apron, right sides together, on the marked edge of the waistband. Match the center of the body of the apron with the center of the waistband. Gather the 40-inch edge to fit the area between the markings on the waistband ends. Pin in place, distributing the gathers as evenly as possible.

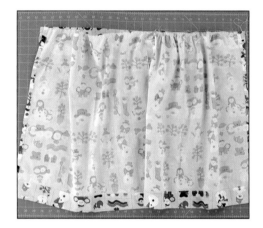

9 Using a ½-inch seam allowance, sew the body of the apron to the waistband.

10 Press as sewn and press with the seam allowance toward the waistband.

11 Fold the unsewn ends of the ties in thirds. Pin into place at ends of the waistband matching right sides of fabric.

12 Fold the waistband over the ties, right sides together, with the ½-inch seam allowance turned upward to enclose the tie. Sew the ends of the waistband even with the ends of the apron body.

CONTINUED ON NEXT PAGE

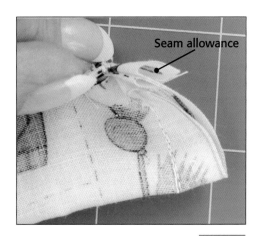

Seam allowance

⑬ Turn the waistband right side out and press.

⑭ Press under ½ inch on unfinished 26-inch edge of waistband.

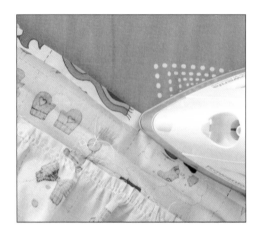

⑮ Match pressed-under edge to the waistband seam and slipstitch in place.

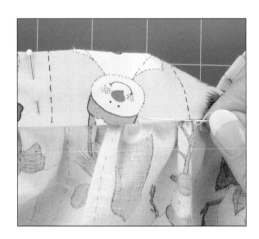

Sheer Fabric Hostess Apron

Try making this sheer apron after you've gained experience working with other fabrics.

MATERIALS
1¼ yard of 45-inch sheer fabric

¼ yard of solid fabric to underline the waistband

Thread to match the fabric

CUTTING
Cut 26 × 3½-inch waistband

Cut two 5 × 32-inch ties

Cut 58 × 24-inch body of the apron

ASSEMBLY

1 Underline the waistband as described on page 239. Follow the directions for the hostess apron. If the fabric you're working with lacks body, apply interfacing to the waistband piece before construction.

2 Sew a 3-inch hem in the body of the apron instead of the 2 inches described in the general directions.

TIP

Use a fine needle for sheer sharp fabric to prevent pulls in the fabric.

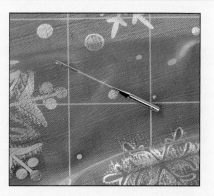

Gathered Bed Skirt

A dust ruffle can hide clutter under the bed in addition to adding color to coordinate home decorating accessories.

Note: Before you cut your fabric, confirm your bed measurements and make adjustments if necessary.

Make the Gathered Bed Skirt

Type of Bed	Standard Size	Platform Fabric (45 Inches Wide)	Dust Ruffle Fabric (45 Inches Wide)
Crib	28 × 52 inches	1½ yards Cut 29 × 53 inches	2½ yards Cut 6, 15½ × 44 inches
Twin	39 × 75 inches	2¼ yards Cut 40 × 76 inches	3½ yards Cut 8, 15½ × 44 inches
Twin X-Long	39 × 80 inches	2⅓ yards Cut 40 × 81 inches	4 yards Cut 9, 15½ × 44 inches
Double	54 × 75 inches	4½ yards of 45-inch wide (2¼ yards of 60-inch wide) Cut 55 × 76 inches	4 yards Cut 9, 15½ × 44 inches
Queen	60 × 80 inches	4⅔ yards Cut 61 × 81 inches	4½ yards Cut 10, 15½ × 44 inches
Standard King	76 × 80 inches	4⅔ yards Cut 77 × 81 inches	4½ yards Cut 11, 15½ × 44 inches
California King	72 × 84 inches	4¾ yards Cut 73 × 85 inches	4¾ yards Cut 11, 15½ × 44 inches

PLATFORM FABRIC

The platform fabric usually lays on the boxspring or frame and holds the dust ruffle in place. For 45-inch fabric on double, queen, and king-size platforms, divide the yardage in half and seam two lengths of fabric to obtain the desired width of the fabric. Trim the joined sections evenly on both sides to achieve the measurements in the chart. A flat sheet can be used to make the platform without having to join fabric. Cut the sheet to the platform measurements.

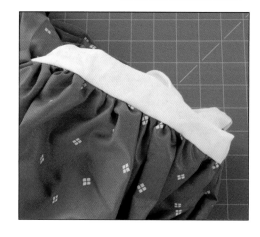

DUST RUFFLE FABRIC

The calculations are for a 45-inch wide cotton woven fabric with approximately double the fabric for gathering. A sheer fabric will require more fabric and a heavy fabric will require less fabric.

All measurements assume a 14-inch drop from the top of the box spring to the floor. For a longer dust ruffle, add to the 15½-inch measurement.

ASSEMBLY

1 Join the strips of dust ruffle fabric on the 15½-inch edges, using a ½-inch seam allowance. To create one long strip, apply a seam finish to the seams.

CONTINUED ON NEXT PAGE

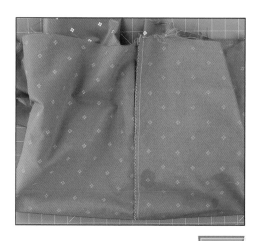

2 Hem the bottom of the dust-ruffle fabric by turning up ½ inch twice and stitching into place. Repeat to hem the ends of the dust ruffle.

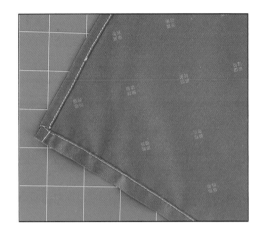

3 Fold the dust ruffle to find the center and quarter marks. Mark the folds on the unsewn edge. Baste the unsewn edge to gather the edge. (See more on gathering in Chapter 6.)

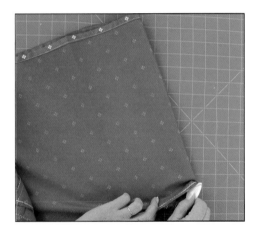

4 Hem one short side end of the platform fabric by turning under ¼ inch twice and stitching it down.

5 Mark the center of the sides and opposite end of the platform fabric.

6 Placing right side down on the right side of platform, match the marks on the platform with the marks on the ruffle. Pin in place at the marks and gather the ruffle to fit the platform edges.

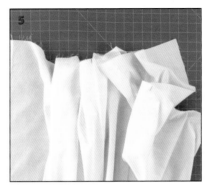

7 Spread the gathers as evenly as possible. Pin the ruffle in place.

8 Sew the platform and ruffle together using a ½-inch seam allowance. Apply a seam finish to the seam allowance.

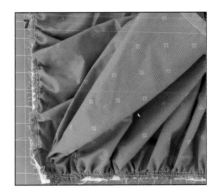

TIP

When gathering a heavy fabric or a large area, try sewing a zigzag stitch over a strong string with quality thread, without sewing the string. Pull the string to gather the fabric.

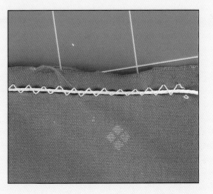

15

Using a Purchased Pattern

You've achieved mastering your sewing machine and understanding basic terms. Now it's time to extend your sewing possibilities! Sewing patterns provide you with a road map to construct a project. You can create anything you want when you combine a pattern with your fabrics and embellishments. Patterns for Halloween costumes, simple clothing items, and home-décor accessories are all good choices for getting started without being overwhelmed with details. There are many patterns on the market for beginners with a wide variety of options.

SINGER

The pattern envelope has all the information you'll need to start and finish your sewing project.

Where to Find Patterns

PATTERN CATALOGS

Your first stop in the fabric store is the pattern catalogs. They're divided into sections, so you can focus on the type of pattern you're looking for. The images in the catalog represent the pattern envelope and contain enough information to help you make a decision.

PATTERNS TO CREATE

The pattern catalogs and the front of the pattern envelopes show you what a pattern can create. Sometimes you have to use your imagination to see the item that *you* want.

ONLINE CATALOGS

Most pattern companies also have their catalogs online, so you can browse from the comfort of home and take your time. These sites are also a wealth of information for fitting problems and alterations.

Once you find the pattern you want, write down the number and the size.

Patterns are usually in large drawers arranged by pattern manufacturers and pattern numbers. This information is listed on the outside of each drawer. Once you've found the correct pattern, you'll need to find the correct size. The patterns should be arranged by size but often are out of order because of customers changing their mind and stuffing patterns back into the drawers.

You can make your own patterns by entering your measurements into a pattern generating software program. The patterns will be made to your exact body measurements. Properly taking measurements is the key to success with computer-generated patterns.

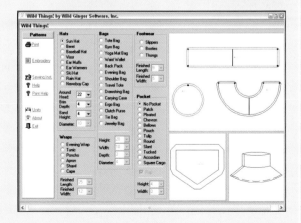

A pattern envelope is much more than a pretty picture to show you what the pattern can create.

Bring It Together

The front of a pattern envelope usually has many views. Each view is labeled with a letter or a number. Choose the number or letter of the item you want to make. For information on pattern sizes, see page 261.

Turn the envelope over to find all the shopping information you need.

One area tells you the pattern number and the number of pieces in the envelope (a).

Fabric suggestions are also included on the envelope (b).

a

9800 — Pattern number

ADULTS' CLOWN COSTUMES AND HAT—14 PIECES: This env
to all costumes listed below.

Fabrics—Cotton types: broadcloth, chambray, muslin, gingham
Neck ruffle also in net, organdy. Extra fabric needed to match pla
and nap layouts for one-way design fabrics. Not suitable for c

BODY MEASUREMENTS
Chest or Bust — Number of — 32:

Sizes — pieces — Sm
32:

b

9800 — Fabric suggestions

ADULTS' CLOWN COSTUMES AND HAT—14 PIECES: This envelope contains pattern pieces an
to all costumes listed below.

Fabrics—Cotton types: broadcloth, chambray, muslin, gingham. Hats also in cotton sateen, cr
Neck ruffle also in net, organdy. Extra fabric needed to match plaids, stripes, one-way designs. Us
and nap layouts for one-way design fabrics. Not suitable for obvious diagonals fabrics.

BODY MEASUREMENTS

		32 34	36 38	40 42
Chest or Bust		Small	Medium	Large
Sizes		32 34	36 38	40 42
	Right half of Top and Left half of Pants 44"-45" *			
New 1 Costume	Left half of Top and Right half of Pants—purchase same amount of contrast fabric as above	2⅝	2⅝	2⅞
	Rick rack—two different colors each color	1⅝	1⅝	2

Many patterns will mention what fabrics are not good choices. Most of the envelope is taken up with a chart that shows you the fabric you'll need to buy.

Choose your size at the top of the chart and the view that you selected on the front of the envelope, on the right side of the chart.

Read the entire area and buy the fabric amount for your size. Notes for contrasting fabrics are also listed in this area. Other yardage requirements may also be listed but not necessarily for each size.

This particular pattern also lists the neck ruffle and hat separately. It's an example of why it is important to read the entire envelope before you leave the store: You want to make sure you buy enough fabric.

Notions you'll need are listed on the pattern envelope, too.

Now you're ready to start your project! Inside the pattern envelope are the pattern pieces and the instructions.

What You'll Find

Open the instruction sheet first. Sketches of the views and the corresponding pattern pieces are detailed.

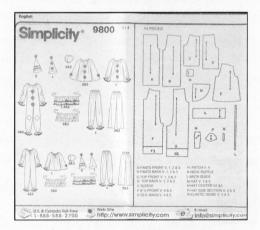

The "General Directions" area explains pattern symbols and construction information. See page 260 for more information.

Almost all patterns have adjustment lines for lengthening or shortening a garment. Always use these lines rather than just add fabric or cut off fabric so that the original lines of the garment are sustained.

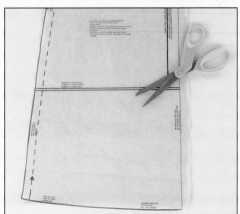

The "Cutting Layouts" are a guide to laying out and cutting your pattern pieces.

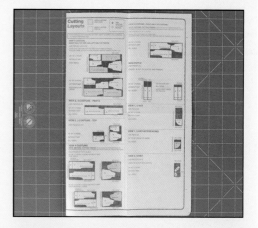

On the instruction sheet, find the area that pertains to the view you've chosen.

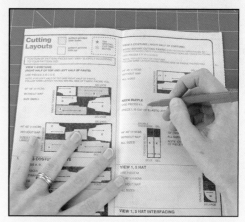

Locate and separate all the pattern pieces you'll need for your project.

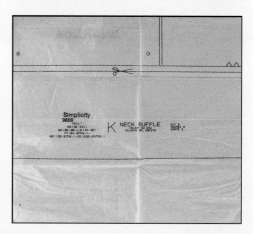

Layout, Cutting, and Marking

Laying out and cutting your fabric may seem like a step you can rush through. But rushing the process can lead to pieces not fitting together when you construct the item. It can also lead to a garment not hanging properly if the grain line is not straight on the grain of the fabric.

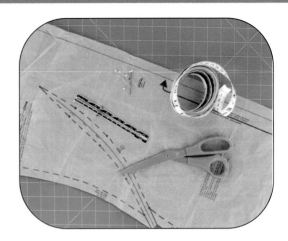

Begin the Process

1. Some patterns are multisized. For these patterns, cut out your desired size or trace the size you want, to preserve all the sizes for future use.

2. Press your pattern pieces with a warm iron and no steam to make them lie flat while pinning.

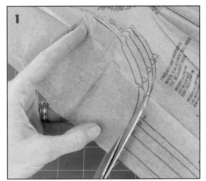

3. Lay your preshrunk and pressed fabric on a flat surface with the pattern pieces required on your layout instructions. The layout will tell you if the fabric should be single- or double-folded. Rough-fit the pattern pieces as they're shown.

4. Some pattern pieces are laid on a fold. The edge line of the pattern is laid right on the fold of the fabric.

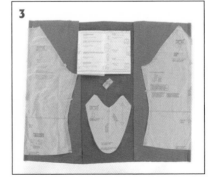
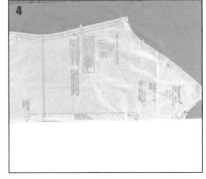

Layout

⑤ Measure the grain line to the selvedge across the length of the grain line marking to be sure the entire pattern piece is straight. Adjust the pattern piece so that the entire grain line is an even distance from the selvedge. Pin the pattern piece on the grain line. Repeat for all pattern pieces. Make sure the pieces don't overlap each other.

⑥ Smoothing the pattern piece from the grain line, pin the edges of the pattern piece to the fabric. Keep the straight pins inside the cutting line.

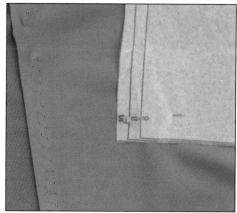

⑦ Make sure the pattern is smooth and flat to the fabric.

CONTINUED ON NEXT PAGE

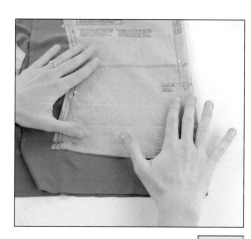

Cutting

8 Now you're ready to cut out the pattern. Sharp scissors are essential to cut a pattern accurately. Cut along the edge of the pattern piece.

9 Keep the fabric and pattern flat on the table as much as possible to prevent the pattern pieces from ripping and for more accurate cutting.

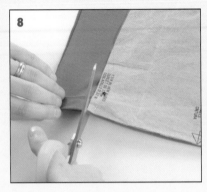

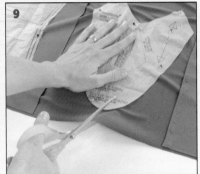

10 Notches are marked in many ways: single (a) or double (b). The best way to preserve your entire seam allowance is to cut the notches out beyond the edge of the pattern piece following the pattern lines.

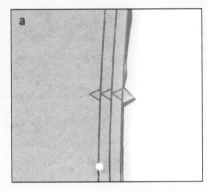

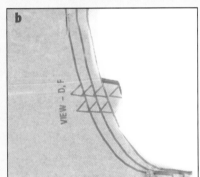

VIEW – D, F

11 When pattern pieces are laid on a fold, the folded edge is not cut open.

12 Cut out all of your pattern pieces and keep the extra fabric for testing stitches on your sewing machine.

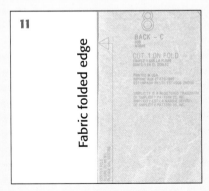

Fabric folded edge

BACK – C

CUT 1 ON FOLD

Marking

13. Mark all dots and make sure that the marks on the fabric are in the same location as they are on the pattern piece. See more on marking on pages 78 and 79.

14. Mark the darts and placement lines. See more on marking darts on page 104.

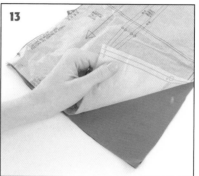

15. Remove the pins from the pattern piece so the fabric is ready for construction but keep the fabric with the pattern piece to identify each part of the pattern.

TIP

If it is difficult to see the difference in the right and wrong side of your fabric, place sticker type dots from a stationary store on the right side of each cut piece to help later when you're constructing the garment. A small marking with tailor's chalk on the wrong side of the fabric will help but is apt to be confused with other pattern markings.

The Instruction Sheet

Following all the steps on the instruction sheet that comes with a pattern ensures that the item will be properly constructed.

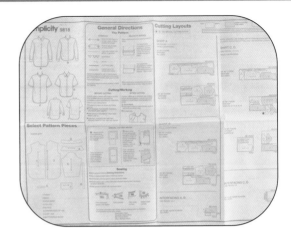

General Directions

① The instruction sheets include general sewing directions. These directions may not have a lot of detail, but you'll have terms you can research if the directions are not clear to you.

② The sewing directions are divided into separate directions for the view you originally chose on the pattern envelope.

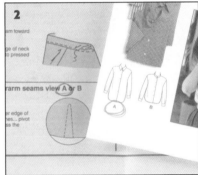

③ Follow the step-by-step directions in the order they are given. Sometimes it is necessary to refer back to previous directions. By going in order, you won't be lost when you run across a reference to previous directions.

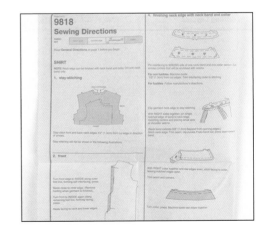

There are large and small pattern companies. You can find patterns from the larger pattern companies at fabric departments within mass merchant stores and in fabric stores. The size you need may vary from company to company.

Determine Your Measurements

Before you leave for the fabric store, take your measurements. Body measurements should be taken over undergarments. All patterns have body measurements to match a pattern size. Here's a sample list of sizes on a misses' pattern.

The **bust measurement** is used to determine the size pattern you should buy for tops, dresses, blouses, jackets, and coats.

The **waist measurement** is used to determine your pattern size for skirts that are not fitted in the hip area.

The **hip measurement** is used to determine your pattern size for pants and fitted skirts.

The **back waist length** is taken by finding the predominant bone at the base of the neck, following the spine to the natural waistline.

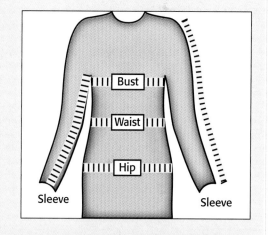

Pattern Industry Standards

Misses' patterns are designed for a well proportioned, developed figure, about 5'5" to 5'6" without shoes.

Size	4	6	8	10	12	14	16	18	20	22	24	26
Bust	29½	30½	31½	32½	34	36	38	40	42	44	46	48
Waist	22	23	24	25	26½	28	30	32	34	37	39	41½
Hip	31½	32½	33½	34½	36	38	40	42	44	46	48	50
Back Waist Length	15½	15½	15¾	16	16¼	16½	16¾	17	17¼	17⅜	17½	17¾

chapter 16

Expanding Your Horizons

This book has been written to get you started and give you the basics to sew and be creative. There is so much available to expand your skills and possibilities, that it could fill an entire library. Once you start sewing the only stop sign is one you put up. Reach out to find people and places to expand your sewing horizons.

SINGER

Stabilizers

Stabilizers are used to temporarily stabilize fabric as you sew. They keep the fabric from puckering or sinking into the throat plate of the sewing machine. Very sheer fabric is the most common fabric to need stabilization when you're sewing seams.

Stabilizers are available in the interfacing section of most fabric stores. Machine embroidery stores also carry a variety of stabilizers.

Stabilize Fabric

Multiple layers of any stabilizer can be used when one layer doesn't achieve the results you're aiming for.

You probably have gift-wrapping tissue paper on hand. Place a layer of the tissue paper under the fabric that wants to pucker. Sew the seam, allowing the tissue paper to be incorporated into the seam. Lengthening the stitch also helps eliminate the puckering. Then simply tear away the tissue paper.

TEAR-AWAY STABILIZER

Tear-away stabilizer is as its name describes. It tears away after stitching very similarly to the way tissue paper tears away.

WATER-SOLUBLE STABILIZER

Water-soluble stabilizer looks like a sheet of cloudy vinyl. Its properties allow it to dissolve in water after the seam is shown.

HEAT-AWAY STABILIZER

Heat-Away stabilizer looks like a loosely woven stiff gauze. It vanishes with the heat of an iron and any remnants of the stabilizer brush away (a). Fabrics that are compatible with the iron are a good choice for using a heat-away type of stabilizer. Fabrics, such as velvet, that require special pressing techniques would *not* be a good choice.

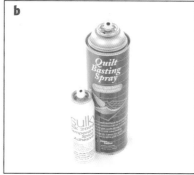

TEMPORARY ADHESIVE

Temporary adhesive is available in a variety of forms. When the fabric wants to slip and slide on the stabilizer, applying temporary adhesive allows the layers of fabric to stay put as you sew (b). Always read the label and follow the manufacturers directions. Test the adhesive on scraps of fabric before you use it on the garment.

Marking Fabric with Tailor Tacks

Tailor tacks are one of the most tried-and-true methods of marking fabric. They were used long before notion companies made life easy with mass-produced marking tools.

Today, tailor tacks are used mainly when other marking methods aren't feasible. For example, you shouldn't use a tracing wheel on a heavy wool fabric because it can cut through and distort the pattern piece as well as possibly leave permanent markings in the fabric.

Mark Fabric with Tailor Tacks

1 Use a hand needle and double thread. You don't have to knot the thread.

2 Sew through the pattern dot or marking, leaving a tail.

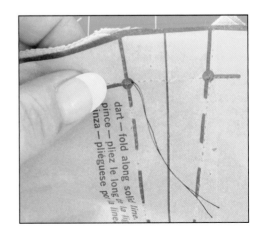

3 Come back through the same spot in the opposite direction, leaving a loop of thread.

4 Repeat by sewing through the first side, leaving a loop. Cut the thread the same length as the loop on the first side.

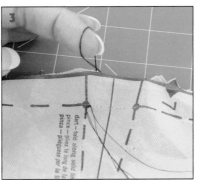 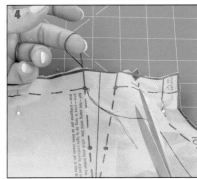

5 Gently hold the thread tails and loops to the fabric and pull the fabric layers apart, so that an even amount of thread is on each side of the fabric. The thread between the fabric, when cut, is approximately the same length as the tails on each side.

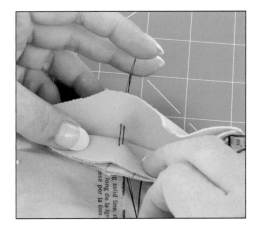

6 Snip the thread that is between the fabric, leaving equal amounts of thread on each side.

7 Snip the loops of thread to have single threads.

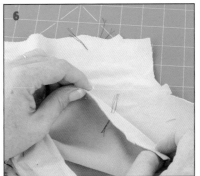 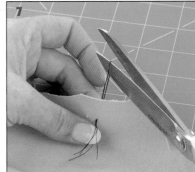

Flat-Felled Seams

Flat-felled or fell seams are commonly seen on jeans. This type of seam is *very* strong and durable. It's sewn by enclosing the entire seam allowance, and it can be sewn on the inside or outside of a garment.

In this sample, we're sewing the flat-felled seam on the outside of the garment.

Make the Flat-Felled Seam

① Sew the seam with the *wrong* sides of the fabric together.

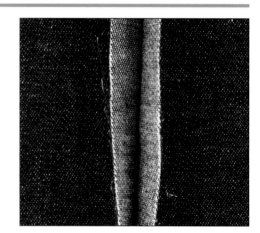

② Press the seam to set the seam and press the seam allowance open.

③ Press the seam to one side.

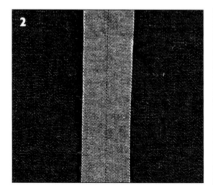

④ Trim away the underneath seam allowance to approximately ⅛ inch from the seam line.

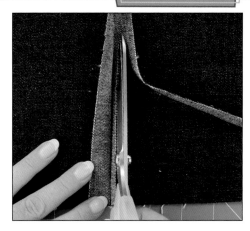

⑤ Fold and press the full seam allowance in half to fold the seam-allowance edge under. It will meet the originally sewn seam when pressed in half.

⑥ Topstitch along the edge of the folded edge to stitch it to the garment.

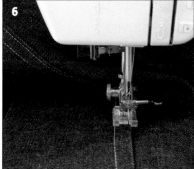

TIP

If the folded seam allowance wants to twist or slip out of place, take the time to baste it in place before sewing it in place.

French Seams

French seams create a very neat seam with the seam allowance enclosed to prevent fraying. They're commonly used on sheer fabric and lace, fabrics that are see-through so the seam finish is actually visible on the finished side of the garment.

Make the French Seam

1. A narrow French seam for a ⅝-inch seam is sewn by sewing a seam with the *wrong* sides of the fabric together. Sew a scant ½-inch seam.

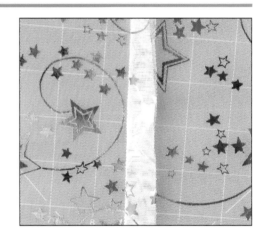

2. Press the seam to one side.

③ Trim the seam allowance to ⅛ inch.

④ Fold and press the right sides of the fabric together, folding along the sewn seam line.

⑤ Sew ⅛ inch from the fold line. This stitching should land on the original seam line. Press seam to one side.

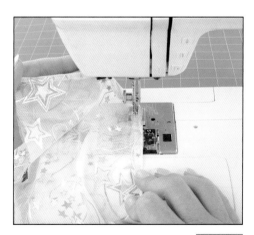

Shortening a Zipper

Whenever you can't find the exact length zipper you want, buy the next longer zipper and shorten it. When you're trying to replace a zipper in a manufactured item, you won't usually find the exact length at the store. Zippers are made to order at the factory or special-ordered in bulk for mass production.

Non-separating Zipper

1. A non-separating zipper is shortened at the bottom of the zipper. Measure the length of the zipper, and mark the length you want.

2. Use your sewing machine to make a bar tack at the marked length. A bar tack is made with a zigzag stitch that goes past both edges of the zipper teeth. The length of the zigzag is shortened so that the stitches are right next to each other. Always test manually to make sure that the needle will clear the zipper teeth before supplying power to the sewing machine.

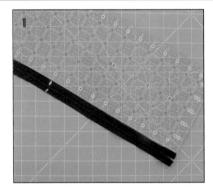

3. Trim the end of the zipper leaving enough tape for installation of the zipper. If possible, remove the teeth beyond the bar tack. If the teeth can't be picked off of the zipper tape, carefully snip them off. Use a zigzag stitch to stabilize the tape where you made the cuts.

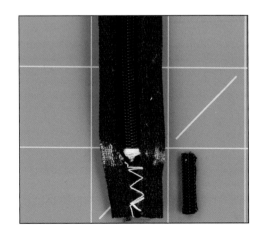

④ A separating zipper is shortened from the top of the zipper so that the retaining box, which holds the bottom of the zipper together, remains intact.

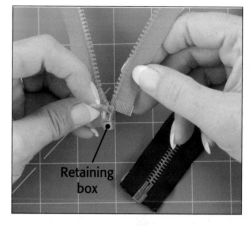

Retaining box

⑤ Measure the zipper, and mark the desired length.

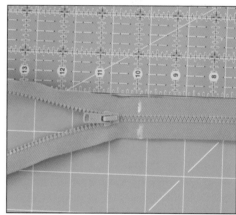

⑥ Leave approximately 1 inch above the mark. If possible, sew the zipper in as normal, folding the top of the zipper over into the seam line. Trim excess after it has been folded to secure the stop from sliding off the end of the zipper.

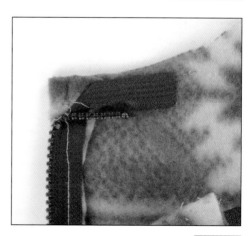

Serger/Overlock Machine Possibilities

A serger, sometimes referred to as an *overlock machine*, provides a professional seam finish.

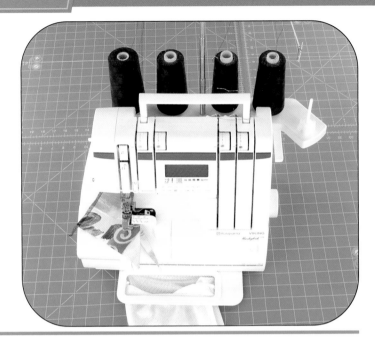

Serged Stitches

Sergers trim the fabric as the threads enclose the seam allowance (a), as well as create a seam that is very stretchable.

These machines can use two, three, four, or five threads to obtain a variety of stitches (b). Seam finishes are the most common use of a serger even though it has so many possibilities. The use of a different number of threads, needle positions, and various tension settings allow the machine to create a wide variety of stitches. As with sewing machines, a wide variety of options are available. The options on a basic serger will not give you all of the stitches that are available on a high-end serger. Visit local dealers and test the options that various machines offer.

Sewing swimwear and other knits on the serger is desirable, especially with the ultimate stretch that a serged seam provides.

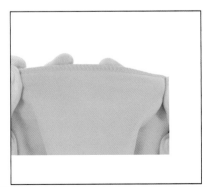

Machine embroidery brings a new meaning to fabric artistry. Embellishments and personalization add flare to any sewn item.

Decorative Stitches

Many machines have an array of specialty decorative stitches. These machines can vary in the size of designs produced, as well as in the number of designs you can sew automatically without changing the settings.

Digital embroidery machines enable you to embroider a full design. With built-in software, you can take any drawing or picture from paper to software and on to the machine to be stitched out.

Once the design is fed to the machine and your fabric is "hooped," the machine automatically moves the fabric to obtain the embroidered design. Designs can be purchased, downloaded from the Internet, combined with other designs, resized, and even made from photographs. The variety is limited only by your imagination.

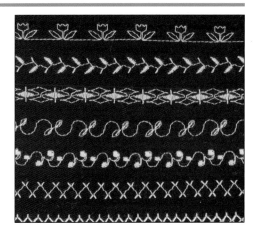

Index

V Visual™ — **Read Less–Learn More®**

Teach Yourself VISUALLY™ books...

Whether you want to knit, sew, or crochet...strum a guitar or play the piano...train a dog or create a scrapbook...make the most of Windows XP or touch up your Photoshop CS2 skills, Teach Yourself VISUALLY books get you into action instead of bogging you down in lengthy instructions. All Teach Yourself VISUALLY books are written by experts on the subject and feature:

• Hundreds of color photos or screenshots that demonstrate each step or skill

• Step-by-step instructions accompanying each photo

• FAQs that answer common questions and suggest solutions to common problems

• Information about each skill clearly presented on a two- or four-page spread so you can learn by seeing and doing

• A design that makes it easy to review a particular topic

Look for Teach Yourself VISUALLY books to help you learn a variety of skills—all with the proven visual learning approaches you enjoyed in this book.

0-7645-9641-1

Teach Yourself VISUALLY™ Crocheting

Picture yourself crocheting accessories, garments, and great home décor items. It's a relaxing hobby, and this is the relaxing way to learn! This Visual guide *shows* you the basics, beginning with the tools and materials needed and the basic stitches, then progresses through following patterns, creating motifs and fun shapes, and finishing details. A variety of patterns gets you started, and more advanced patterns get you hooked!

0-7645-9640-3

Teach Yourself VISUALLY™ Knitting

Get yourself some yarn and needles and get clicking! This Visual guide *shows* you the basics of knitting—photo by photo and stitch by stitch. You begin with the basic knit and purl patterns and advance to bobbles, knots, cables, openwork, and finishing techniques—knitting as you go. With fun, innovative patterns from top designer Sharon Turner, you'll be creating masterpieces in no time!

0-7645-9642-X

Teach Yourself VISUALLY™ Guitar

Pick up this book and a guitar and start strumming! *Teach Yourself VISUALLY Guitar* shows you the basics photo by photo and note by note. You begin with essential chords and techniques and progress through suspensions, bass runs, hammer-ons, and barre chords. As you learn to read chord charts, tablature, and lead sheets, you can play any number of songs, from rock to folk to country. The chord chart and scale appendices are ready references for use long after you master the basics.

designed for visual learners like you!

0-7645-7927-4

Teach Yourself VISUALLY™ Windows® XP, 2nd Edition

Clear step-by-step screenshots *show* you how to tackle more than 150 Windows XP tasks. Learn how to draw, fill, and edit shapes, set up and secure an Internet account, load images from a digital camera, copy tracks from music CDs, defragment your hard drive, and more.

0-7645-8840-0

Teach Yourself VISUALLY™ Photoshop® CS2

Clear step-by-step screenshots *show* you how to tackle more than 150 Photoshop CS2 tasks. Learn how to import images from digital cameras, repair damaged photos, browse and sort images in Bridge, change image size and resolution, paint and draw with color, create duotone images, apply layer and filter effects, and more.

Available wherever books are sold.

Wiley, the Wiley logo, the Visual logo, Read Less-Learn More, and Teach Yourself Visually are trademarks or registered trademaiks of John Wiley & Sons, Inc. and/or its affiliates.
All other trademarks are the property of their respective owners.

Visual®
An Imprint of WILEY
Now you know.